YOUR GUIDE TO FLORIDA PROPERTY INVESTMENT

Owning, Investing & Enjoying
the Florida Lifestyle

FOR GLOBAL BUYERS

Written by Lisa and Lee Mirman

Edited by Natalie Revie

WHO WE ARE

Lee and Lisa Mirman both hold their MBA from Duke University and between them have more than thirty years' experience in Florida real estate. Their market-leading real estate firm, Investments in Sarasota, wins the five star award "Best in Client Satisfaction" year after year. Together they travel the world, gathering global perspective of their clients' needs and motivating factors. Their extensive know-how and confidence in the security and opportunity of the Florida real estate market has manifested in establishing their own real estate investment fund for foreign investors.

Lee is a licensed real estate broker with an extensive background in finance, economics, and venture capital. He worked on Wall Street at Chase Manhattan Bank, and has founded multiple ventures in the US, Europe and Latin America. Because of his strategic vision and ethics he has been honoured by the US Congress as a "Hero of Small Business". Lee has presented around the world as one of the foremost expert on Florida real estate investment.

Lisa brings a mastery in marketing, communications, and technology. She also has an award-winning corporate and start-up track record. She is a licensed real estate professional and for more than a decade has worked to implement leading-edge international marketing strategies as well as sales processes to optimally serve the brokerage's real estate clients. Lisa is fluent in Spanish and holds an undergraduate degree from the top-ten ranked University of Chicago.

Lee and Lisa love living in Sarasota, Florida with their two children and Bernese Mountain dog. As seasoned yoga practitioners, they are committed to their own continual expansion in mind, body and spirit. They are also enthusiastic advocates of the principles of environmental consciousness, holistic health and wellness, and mindful living.

Who in the WORLD are YOU?

Throughout most of this book we refer to citizens from outside the United States who come to invest in our real estate market as GLOBAL buyers. We use the word GLOBAL because we feel it has a very positive and welcoming ring to it. We occasionally may also use FOREIGN or INTERNATIONAL. As you are reading other resources, particularly for the purpose of immigration and visas, you may also encounter the term ALIEN. All these are words are used interchangeably in English.

Here's to knowing all you need to know to go forth and buy!

ACKNOWLEDGEMENTS

The greatest joy in our work comes from developing long-term relationships with clients from all over the world. We truly appreciate the colour and perspectives each of you has brought into our personal and professional lives. It is thrilling to be your partner in real estate as we continually learn by serving you through each distinct transaction. Also, we find it immeasurably rewarding to see the joy the Florida lifestyle brings to your families, in whatever fashion that translates to for you.

We are delighted to thank those professionals with whom we have learned and grown together over the last many years. It is their expertise and integrity, along with the time we have shared "in the trenches", that has primed us with the knowledge and experience to write this guide.

Robert S. Ludwig, President, Ludwig-Walpole Insurance Agency

Juan C. Villaveces, Board Certified Real Estate Attorney & Partner, Shumaker, Loop & Kendrick, LLP

Sean W. Martin, Owner/President, Martin Funding

Shelly Parmet-Evans, CPA and Principle, Piper, Hawkins & Company

In addition, we have two extraordinary mentors whose gifts are not specific to real estate, but whose wisdom has guided us to a place of conscious, abundant, and healthy living:

Linda Sherr, for illuminating our personal and professional path through life with unrelenting dedication to our growth, peace, and clarity.

Dr. Sharon La Rosa, for her ever-present support of our whole family to ensure our vibrant health and holistic well-being.

Thank you, **Natalie Revie**, our friend, colleague and editor, whose talents transcend many disciplines. We honour your capabilities in the many realms in which you have supported us, and look forward to many more fruitful engagements with you in the future!

Finally, we honour the pivotal role the love and support of our families has played throughout our lives, and here share our endless gratitude for how they sculpted us into the people we are today! Namaste.

TABLE OF CONTENTS

FOREWORD

Historically, Florida has always been a global favourite with property investors and holiday makers alike. A large part of Florida's appeal lies in its wonderful sub-tropical climate, Caribbean waters, and sunshine. There will always be an abundance of people looking for holiday homes, vacation rentals, and to spend time in the sunshine state, escaping colder climates elsewhere. This—along with favourable tax laws and guarantees on property ownership—gives the Florida property market a solid and secure foundation. And makes it not only a great investment and a great financial choice for your primary residence should you choose, but an unbeatable lifestyle choice overall, in our opinion.

In recent times of economic turbulence, some great opportunities to achieve value have been presented—whether by fluctuating home currencies giving foreign buyers a price advantage—or property prices falling and offering ultra-affordable Florida lifestyle. Savvy investors have taken the leap to move their money, to what *was* a slightly distressed market after the property bubble burst. Now, as the market recovers and finds its equilibrium, there are still opportunities to be had. And for international investors with the right information at their fingertips, there are some great opportunities to achieve both long-term financial returns, and a piece of our priceless Florida lifestyle.

While Florida has always been able to play the weather card, and we don't doubt there will always be plentiful customers for the wares which Florida offers, we do feel that there are large numbers of people who jump in to the Florida property market either ill-informed, ill-advised, or both. It's a huge state, and there are myriad micro-markets which need to be understood intimately in order to make the ideal property choice for you. You need to consider not only your investment dollars, but your family's needs and the lifestyle you desire. Balancing these factors is an art form, one we're adept at. But all-too-often we see buyers from abroad falling prey to unscrupulous or incompetent agents, Realtors, or insurance vendors—and subsequently making poor decisions purely based on lack of information or mis-information.

In this guide we will provide a wealth of information gleaned over three decades in the Florida property market. We'll endeavour to steer you through the choppy waters of making an international real estate purchase in the state of Florida, so you understand each step, and are better able to make smart decisions which allow you to enjoy all the wonderful things that come along with purchasing a slice of the Florida dream.

We will also strive to find the right Realtor to represent you in your search, through the **Investments in Florida Realtor Referral Program** at *www.InvestmentsInFlorida.com,* a referral network of personally vetted real estate professionals. These are professionals in their field whom we believe to be the best in their particular areas of business. Above all, we want to provide good, solid, information, so that when you come to make a property choice you're doing so from an informed position with good knowledge of the processes involved, the pitfalls to be aware of, and the right questions to ask of everybody involved: from your Realtor and inspectors, to your vendors, and closing agent.

We've been in this game for a long time—35 years in fact. We've seen it all: from people making the right property investment, which will grow and accumulate equity for their children's and grandchildren's futures, right through to people who've been taken advantage of, had poor information, and lost as much as half a million dollars in a single year on a home they bought. Above all, what 40 years have taught us is that knowledge is power. And in real estate, knowledge is gold dust. We hope this guide will help you going forward as an informed, savvy real estate investor.

The Problem of Dis-Information

Everyone is in the information business. And consumers nowadays like to drink up information as if it is water and they just finished a 10-hour desert hike. Now everyone is an expert at everything. The problem is that most of the information being consumed is inaccurate, and most of the people selling or sharing the information are misinformed themselves. Recently, we were corrected by one of our newsletter readers whose unique circumstance wasn't applicable to our general statement. After doing "extensive" research she found an answer more suited to her needs. And therein lies the conundrum: is everyone's situation that unique or do they just think it is? For most people the answer is no: their situation *has* been experienced before. Yes, there are twists, nuances, and turns, but an expert will have the experience to find the solution. A lot of solutions have been created, we each do not need to recreate the wheel.

What we need to do is to seek out the advice and guidance of people who are really good at what *they* do and can provide the solution to the problem. We are in the relationship business and we stress multiple times each day that we work with people who we know, like and trust AND who possess *proven* expertise. The point is that as you contemplate your next real estate purchase in the United States, and in Florida in particular, it is critical to get good advice for this transaction, and this information may be different from your last purchase in Florida or your next purchase in Florida. It needs to be current, relevant, and on the money; information only an expert, not articles or internet searching, can provide.

This kind of nuanced advice is based on much more than a one-size-fits-all generalization. It's based on what you are buying, your expectations for ownership, and your own life circumstances at the moment. Is this property for investment? Or a place for your kids to live while attending university in the U.S.? Is it to rent now and live in later? Are all of your kids grown now, whereas your last purchase was when you were vacationing together? Perhaps you have considerably more money than you did previously?

This book will help you establish a baseline understanding of the current state of the market and give you the knowledge to go forward with confidence. Our mantra in business is to get good information so that we can make informed choices. We meet too many people who made the wrong choice because of bad information—sometimes the fault of others and sometimes their own—or by not following their instincts. Remember, everyone is the information business and has something to sell. Your job is to get the best information available that pertains to your situation.

The Briefest History of Florida

We are not historians, so we'll make this quick. In 2013 Florida celebrated 500 years of its first real estate transactions. Ok, that is not necessarily the case, and we are sure that there are many interpretations of the story! Spanish colonists established the city of St. Augustine in 1565, but early explorations are recorded in the area as early as 1513—way ahead of the celebrated pilgrim forefathers who would make their landings in the North Eastern United States much later in 1620. As was the case in the bloody history of the New World, it was a brutal situation of first-come-first-served. If you came by boat to discover a place, the fact there were indigenous populations was irrelevant, because they weren't visible. You claimed it as your own.

The Spanish colonists ruled the state from St Augustine, which formed part of the Viceroyalty of New Spain, Cuba and the Spanish Empire until 1763, when Spain traded Florida to the British in exchange for the return of Cuba to Spanish possession. At the end of the Revolutionary War in 1783 Britain ceded control of most of Florida back to the Spanish. Florida finally became part of the United States in 1819 when the U.S. and Spain signed a treaty handing Florida to the U.S. Eventually Florida gained its statehood in 1845, becoming the 27th of the United States, and modern Florida was born—with a mish-mash of cultures, religions and histories which are still in evidence today.

WHY INVEST IN FLORIDA?

Lifestyle: Living in America & Cultural Familiarity

The opportunity to live in the United States for many people is a long-time dream, offering not only political stability, economic opportunity and security, but world-class education and medicine, some of the most spectacular wonders of the world, and financial incentives for businesses and entrepreneurs. In addition, for a lot of people choosing to buy Florida real estate, there is some cultural familiarity with Florida—whether from speaking the language, having family here, or having vacationed extensively in the state. Over 44 percent of the population of Florida is from European descent, it is the third most populous state in the U.S., and it is the top visitor destination in the United States: which means there is often an underlying familiarity for most people from Europe and Latin America. Remember, purchasing in Florida is also an investment in lifestyle. Life in Florida is relatively easy compared to many places in the world, and the lifestyle is one of the best on earth, in our opinion.

Location & Climate

The real reason people come to Florida to buy and own property is because, for 60 percent of the year, the weather is better here than many of the alternatives. No ice to slip on, no clouds and grey, and lots of activities year-round. Plus 1,200 miles of coastline, and 663 miles of beaches to enjoy.

North and central Florida are sub-tropical, and south Florida is tropical. This means most of Florida enjoys temperatures between 10 and 33 degrees Celsius year round and has year round, swimmable, crystal clear waters. This contributes more than just a pleasant climate: it also affects the economy of the state significantly.

This is important for real estate investors to consider: areas which experience steady and consistent growth are more likely to perform steadily as an investment. And Florida—thanks to its sunny climate—enjoys an excellent rental market and influx of tourists every year, as well as a steady flow of retirees and second homeowners looking to escape the more miserable winters in other parts of the United States, or the world. In addition to the favourable climate and 300 plus days of sunshine a year, Florida is also easily accessible from most international destinations, and boasts a wealth of natural attractions as well as many world-famous man-made tourist attractions.

While Disney is—and always will be—a fantastic draw for the state, sometimes Florida's splendour gets overlooked in its global marketing and perception. Many people we meet when we travel around the world are surprised to learn that in addition to meeting the famous mouse, they can also swim with dolphins, watch manatees swimming in our waters, and experience the glorious peace of our everglades—one of the most diverse eco systems on earth. This is the Florida which speaks to hearts, the Florida which is sometimes overlooked, and the Florida which—in our opinion—converts holiday-makers into buyers, residents, and investors in our incredible state.

Financial: Holding Investments in U.S. Dollars

For many people there is a strong financial factor to their decision to buy here, in addition to the lifestyle benefits. As a starting point, owning real estate in the United States allows two things: Investment in the real estate asset class as well as holding the investment in U.S. dollars. Florida then offers additional sweeteners to its real estate buyers: no personal state income tax, and homestead protection for its residents. Add to that title insurance on your home—so no one can contest your ownership (effectively your ownership of the home is insured)—and full transparency in real estate transactions, and you have an attractive package.

Transparency

In the U.S. real estate transactions are very transparent. This is why we place the emphasis on finding the Realtor first. A new listing for sale is required to be posted to the multiple listing service within 24 hours so that active listings are available to all agents. This is unlike in many other countries where buyers have to go from agent to agent to find a property. Each Realtor has access to all the listings in their local geography and can assist you in the purchase of any one of them.

FLORIDA HAS NO PERSONAL STATE INCOME TAX!!!

Florida is one of the very few states in the United States that does not assess a personal income tax on its residents. This means should you take a job or earn rental income in Florida, you will save by not paying state tax on your income. This is a huge draw for global as well as U.S. buyers. We have a number of clients who establish residency in Florida as it saves them lots of tax dollars. We must be clear that you still need to pay federal income taxes.

THE ECONOMY OF FLORIDA

Florida's economy is becoming more robust, with many major companies and U.S. national corporations making their bases in the state. This gives the entire economy a boost, with high levels of employment in comparison to many other states, higher than average income ratio, and more money spent on entertainment and leisure.

The Gross Domestic Product of the state has continued to grow steadily throughout the recession years. All these factors combine to make Florida a good place to put your money. The tourism economy is also growing year on year.

In 2012, the number of tourists visiting Florida grew by 2.3 percent on the previous year to a record-breaking 89.3 million visitors. Also marking the second year in a row Florida has increased its visitors by over 2 million people. That's a pretty impressive performance after the global economic uncertainty in many other industries over the past five years.

Increases in funding for the state-backed 'Visit Florida' campaign are the result, with the aim of making Florida the number one place to visit in the world. And all this is great news for investors, as international visitors also increased by nine percent to over 10 million. We think you'd struggle to find a more sound economy, or location, to invest in worldwide at this current time.

SOME STATISTICS RELATING TO INDUSTRY IN FLORIDA

- Florida is a hub for the life sciences with 1,000 Biotech and Pharmaceutical companies based in the state and a new "Medical City" for consumers, called Lake Nona, under construction just outside Orlando

- Florida is the second largest state for aerospace and aviation, with 2,000 companies operating

- Information Technology is a huge sector in the Florida economy with 25,000 IT companies in the state

- Florida's largest sector of Financial and Professional Services consists of 122,000 companies.[1]

PROPERTY PRICES

With housing prices in most areas falling during the global economic crisis, Florida homes often became extremely affordable in comparison to other countries. In particular, the quality of life offered for the "price" seems to be truly exceptional for many people compared to what they get at home. During the period in which the market was very distressed—i.e. when some people owed more on their homes than they were worth—there were dramatically affordable homes coming onto the market, presenting opportunities for foreign cash buyers.

As the market has stabilized there are fewer of these properties, which is good for the health of our economy, and also means that the bulk cash buyers from abroad—who were buying up swathes of property and inflating prices— have turned to other more distressed markets to find their bargains. This is good for international buyers looking now, as prices—while stable—are not escalating quite as fast as they were in the last 12 months, buoyed up by institutional buyers. Property bought now is at a fair and stable value, appreciating steadily, and over the long-term—as long as you buy the right home—it will always earn you a good return.

Prices are still nowhere near as high as at their peak in 2005, so you are still getting good value if you compare what you can afford now, to what you could have bought seven years ago. And, while you can't time the market, some global buyers are the beneficiaries of their currency's strength against the dollar. Even so, buyers should make sure the price tag of the property they're purchasing offers real value for money, and is appropriate based on comparisons in the local market, recent sales, and the value of key features. The only way to be sure of this, as we've said before, is to make sure you have a Realtor whose local knowledge and experience is excellent.

CASE STUDIES

CASE STUDY ONE: INVESTOR/HOLIDAYMAKER

Mark and Emily Brightman, and their daughters aged eight, six and two are from Berkshire in England. They want to use the home for three weeks in the summer, and two weeks over Christmas, and rent it the rest of the time. They want to be within two hours drive of the major Disney attractions, and half an hour or less from a beach. Once the kids are older Emily and Mark may spend half the year as retirees.

OUR ADVICE A lot of people think a good location is being in a place where you can have easy access to places you want to go. In Florida, trying to have the best of both worlds may mean you end up in the middle of nowhere. Our advice is to make a choice: what is the most important lifestyle factor for you? For a family with young kids it's undoubtedly the beach. They may well go to Disneyworld a few times a year, but they will want to access and utilize the beach the entire time they're on their Florida vacation. And thankfully there are some fantastic beach communities which still offer you reasonable commute time to the attractions which have made Florida famous.

If you choose east coast beaches, you're looking at bigger waves, beautiful Atlantic sunrises and a more dramatic coastline. If you choose the west coast, you'll be on the Gulf of Mexico, a calmer body of water with more gentle inclines to the water access, and beautiful sunsets. Either way, each and every beach community you look at will offer you unique characteristics in livability and lifestyle, and that's what you should be focusing on. This family should also make sure they choose a property which allows weekly rental to maximize their cash flow potential, and should see an accountant to make sure their tax returns on the rental profit are all filed neatly. They should also be aware that it's possible to deduct the cost of coming to visit the rental from the tax payable on the rental income.

CASE STUDY 2: STRAIGHT INVESTOR

Hans is German, he has $500,000 to invest and wants to get his money in a U.S. asset immediately. He's looking for a good value investment that will rent quickly and consistently with a solid cash flow return, and appreciation over five years. He does not want to come to the U.S. or deal with any more paperwork than he has to.

OUR ADVICE We would advise Hans to think very carefully about his long-term goals, and why he wants property in the U.S. Apart from wanting his money in U.S. assets, does he—like many European clients we've met—only want his money to be in property? If not, and he's looking for straight return, he may want to investigate stocks, shares or other options. If he really does want to own a Florida home, it's worth thinking long term, as with that amount of money he could investigate becoming a Green Card holder and getting residency in the U.S. If he really just wants to own real estate as an investment, then we'd advise him to purchase something which will make a good annual rental. That way he has the solid income stream he wants; there is less wear and tear on the property, and fewer complications of turnover to deal with. He can organize a property manager to take care of everything, and find a good long term tenant. His strategy should be to buy in the best possible location to maximize cash flow in the short term, and appreciation over the longer term, which will be the more important return in the end. Hans may also benefit from the recent currency rates between the euro and the dollar. Eurozone buyers got eight percent more for their money in 2013 compared to 2012.

CASE STUDY 3: RELOCATOR

Manuel and his wife, Carmen, from Venezuela are relocating to Florida for Carmen's job. They will have a five year working/residency visa, and want a property that is within an hour's commute of a major international airport, is easy to maintain, and will sell easily should they choose to return to Venezuela. They would also like to be near the beach, and have the potential to rent the property should they choose to at the end of five years.

OUR ADVICE

With over 1200 miles of coastline and 600 plus miles of beaches in Florida to choose from, we would advise Carmen and Manuel to focus on the lifestyle they want to achieve. There is plenty of opportunity to achieve a wonderful beach-centric lifestyle with all the accessibility and ease they desire. There are 15 international airports in the state, so it shouldn't be hard to tick that box, what they need to know clearly is what kind of lifestyle they would like. Being near the water and beach is part of the culture here, and should be a focal point of their Florida experience.

Each community will have slightly different lifestyles and differentiators, so they need to get really clear on what it is they're looking for. If it's South American flair then South Florida might be more their speed, if it's more temperate climate and resort communities then the area from Sarasota to Tampa may be right for them. The best thing to do is speak to one of our consultants to help identify the lifestyle they're after. A condo might be a good option for them as they're looking for ease of ownership, and these are carefree and low maintenance. However there are many planned communities that offer condo convenience in single family homes. There may be basic fees for maintenance, garden, pool, etc. right through to concierge services who will stock your fridge and put fresh flowers in your home. Florida is service orientated and there are plenty of amenities at your disposal, we are geared towards ease of lifestyle.

4 MOST IMPORTANT THINGS TO REMEMBER WHEN BUYING FLORIDA REAL ESTATE

1. **Location, Location, Location.** The location is the most important factor that will determine both the long-term potential of your property purchase, and your personal enjoyment when using the property. In other words: go

for the best you can possibly afford in terms of desirable location, and it will pay off long term through better occupancy rates, long term appreciation, and your own personal lifestyle. Don't be tempted to go for a cheaper property because you get more space, or percentage-wise you think the return will be higher because the investment is lower. Go for the best location you can afford, as close to the beach as you can, and you will be protecting your investment. Desirable commands a premium, so while it might hurt paying it, it won't hurt receiving it.

2. **Trust Your Instincts** If the property doesn't feel quite right to you, whether in terms of setting, view, or neighbourhood, then walk away. No matter what "deal" or price incentive may be offered, if it isn't right for you, it isn't right, period.

3. **Spend Up Front for Protection** In our eyes it's better to spend a bit of money upfront to make sure that you are protected as an international buyer. This might mean creating legal structures, or money management portfolios, or visa applications, or insurance, but it's best to get everything in place upfront so you are protecting your asset and your income stream.

4. **Find People You Trust** Do your due diligence on them, and then follow their advice or guidance. Once you find people you trust you have to be prepared to defer to

their expertise. Often people close to you will give well meaning advice, but they are not experts, and you need to be prepared to place your trust in the experts you hire to get the best outcome.

CHAPTER

YOUR FLORIDA PROPERTY SEARCH

THE FLORIDA
PROPERTY MARKET

Like the rest of America, Florida experienced record
price growth in the property market in the years leading
up to 2006. In our estimation the market peaked in 2005,
and by late 2005 prices were falling. Of course it takes
time for that information to make itself apparent, become
general knowledge, and to filter out into the marketplace.
Unfortunately, some buyers were still purchasing at a
premium at that time, and were among the worst stung by
the subsequent plummeting of prices in 2006. Some of these
unfortunate buyers were the victims of—in our opinion—

poor advice from their Realtors. Some were just enamoured of the property and wanted it, period. And some just didn't do their homework. Sadly the result for many was negative equity in their homes at the very least, and for others the pain of making a distressed sale, or being foreclosed upon, or perhaps having to take a loss of $200,000 to $500,000, or more.

This gross readjustment of the market was in some ways inevitable after the inflationary behaviour of the market in preceding years—a classic bubble. And as we emerged from the crisis and started to find stability in 2012, you could say that the values attributed to properties became more accurate. Crazy inflationary growth is no more, so homes are being valued based on historical data, and what their assets are truly worth to the buyer. A much more authentic and accurate market is what we're left with today.

This, in our opinion, is no bad thing. And for investors from abroad who are looking to purchase Florida investment property, this is a good time to get some real value on a Florida real estate investment. Prices are still historically low—but they are stable and in most areas rising. This means there is the security of knowing that a property you buy today will be worth more tomorrow. While we're not talking about the rocketing property values as we saw in those boom years, there is steady value to be accumulated in properties bought wisely now. And prices are, we think, fair and accurate.

As this recent article from The Financial Post indicates, things are changing, and opportunities we're seeing in the current market won't be around for long. This article is especially relevant for Canadian buyers, who are well placed in currency terms to buy now, but in our opinion holds true for most international investors, and is generally sound advice:

"A 2012 report from BMO indicates that while the housing market in Florida is relatively stressed, the worst is over. Florida was one of the epicentres of the housing bubble-bust cycle, but there are mounting signs that a recovery is under way. Most savvy real estate investors will tell you the best time to buy is just when the market has turned a corner and is starting to go up—and that's where Florida is now."[2]

Opportunity for Global Buyers

For the global buyer this presents a very real opportunity as—depending on the country and currency you're coming from—the dollar, the price of borrowing, and the price of property ownership may well all be significantly lower than in your country of origin. Add to that the significant potential in most areas of Florida to rent your holiday home for an income, and in many cases an excellent return on your investment and you can see why the Florida property market is an attractive investment for overseas buyers. As well as the attractive prospect of putting their investment money in U.S. dollars, according to the National Association of Realtors: "Foreign buyers recognize U.S. real estate as a desirable, profitable and secure investment. In addition, the weak dollar has made U.S. real estate an even more attractive investment for foreign buyers."[3]

In 2010, international clients in Florida represented an estimated 22 percent of existing home purchases. In 2012, international buyers purchased $82.5 billion in residential real estate in the U.S.—an increase from $53.4 billion two years previously. In Miami, 60 percent of home buyers were from overseas last year according to the Miami Association of Realtors. These are astounding numbers, and demonstrate just how hot the Florida real estate market is right now, particularly for European, Canadian, and Latin American buyers.

One caveat though: This is true at this moment. It is a window of opportunity. If there's one thing our combined experience on Wall Street, in global business and international finance, and our Duke MBAs have taught us it's that no one can say for how long any given situation will exist. Interest rates, currency values, and the property market itself are always in flux and subject to changes and shifts at any time. Right now, we see a significant chance for many international investors to make a good, solid investment in the market and enjoy both the financial and lifestyle returns of owning a Florida holiday home for years, if not decades, to come.

A WORD FROM THE EXPERT

 "Prices won't likely go lower" says Beata Caranci, deputy chief economist at Toronto-Dominion Bank. "If you were trying to get in at the very bottom, you missed it. You are still pretty darn close to skimming the bottom, and the more you wait, you can expect about 5% price growth every year."[4]

Real Estate vs. Other Assets

IS REAL ESTATE REALLY A SOUND INVESTMENT VERSUS OTHER ASSET CLASSES?

Because of the major adjustment in the value of real estate between 2006 and 2011 many buyers are nervous that real estate is no longer a sound and secure investment. Physically owning real estate still, in our opinion, presents one of the safest places to invest your money for a number of reasons:

1. The perhaps most persuasive reason for real estate over other assets, is that you get to use it. Unlike stocks and bonds where there is no tangible use for the products in your daily life, Florida property as an investment is also to be enjoyed.

2. Despite having just been through the bursting of a bubble, historically when viewed over a decade or so, values always go up

3. Owning property can build an excellent store of equity and value, protecting your portfolio against inflation

4. Rental properties can provide great yearly returns and desirable cash income for investors

5. Interest rates are historically low right now, which indicates a rise could be about to happen. This is worrying for investors holding fixed income investments like bonds, which could be negatively impacted by a hike in interest rates

6. There are usually some forms of tax breaks when investing in real estate. In Florida there are tax breaks for depreciation, mortgage payments, and rental income. In fact in Florida the tax savings on real estate investments can be significant

7. The best time to put your money in real estate is when interest rates are low, and the economy is not at full strength. Financing intelligently may mean when the market rises and rates go up, real estate prices rise accordingly, and you are sitting pretty having created equity

8. Real estate is often considered a good investment during inflationary periods which some economists are able to predict.

In fact due to the extreme instability in other traditional investment asset classes such as stocks and shares, we now believe that real estate offers one of the most solid investment opportunities out there. And we think that a lot of investors are making the jump to real estate as they try to escape the traditional equity market, which in recent years has become like playing with fire.

Obviously investing in real estate carries risk—and it is not as liquid as other assets. Which means it is more difficult to cash in should you need to access the equity quickly. Some of the other issues that may arise when owning property as an investment are listed below, and discussed in later sections in this book. All are points worth thinking about. However, we feel that long-term investing in real estate in most cases has the highest financial and personal payoff. Nothing beats the feeling of enjoying the sunshine from your very own Florida home.

Things to Consider

ACTUAL COST OF OWNERSHIP INCLUDES:

- Maintenance Fees - Repairs

- Rental management costs – Agency

- Homeowner Association Fees

- Utilities

- Insurance

- Property taxes

- Tax on rental income

PERSONAL COST OF OWNERSHIP:

- Property management headaches if you do it yourself – dealing with repairs/contractors/services/insurance claims should they arise

- Tenant headaches if you handle the rental yourself— Time and energy spent on logistics and booking.

Types of Investment

WAYS TO INVEST:

1. Holiday Home for Your Family

2. Holiday Home for Holiday Rental Cash Flow Return

3. Condos

4. Holiday Home for Long-term Rental

5. Commercial Property

6. Timeshares/Managed Communities

7. Land

One Final Option for Investing in Real Estate

Another way of owning real estate is by investing in securities which are backed by real estate properties. You can do this by buying stocks, bonds, or real estate investment trusts, mortgage-backed securities or commercial mortgage-backed securities. This does require a level of investment savvy, and an understanding of the real estate which is securing the bonds, so that you can be sure of the stability of the investment and the cash flow. This may be easier than owning real estate outright, and very often is a much less significant investment, which makes it attractive to investors with smaller means.

Common Questions and Concerns from Global Buyers

AS A NON-U.S. CITIZEN, CAN WE OWN PROPERTY IN THE U.S? AND HOW DO WE GO ABOUT BUYING IT?

Fortunately for the global real estate investor eyeing up a piece of Florida real estate, there are no restrictions on foreigners purchasing and owning real estate in the U.S. However it's up to the purchaser to determine if their home country puts any restrictions on buying abroad. It's worth really investigating this, as some countries can discourage foreign investment outside their own shores through punitive taxes on purchasing real estate abroad, or restricting the amount of time residents can spend outside of their home country without losing residency rights.

Many people choose Florida property as an investment, either as a part-time residence, as an income-generating rental, and/or as a future retirement property. In all these scenarios it is very important to check any restrictions that may be in place in your home country whether via taxes, financial, or visas.

It's worth noting that buying real estate in the U.S. is one of the safest investment destinations you can choose. All real estate transactions are protected by U.S. contract law. And the use of Escrow as a standard protects your money while a transaction is in progress.

DO WE HAVE TO BE IN THE U.S. TO BUY REAL ESTATE?

No. It's advisable to view your property in person, but if you choose not to be present your agent can act on your behalf to both view the property and do the deal. And when it comes to closing you don't need to be present, you have the option to give 'Power of Attorney' to a representative who can close the deal for you. Or, as we're finding, more and more real estate sales are being closed virtually, with all of the original documents being signed abroad and then being sent back to the U.S. If you are signing the papers in your own country, you don't need to give power of attorney to anybody else, and we have even had cases of lawyers traveling abroad to witness the signature. Please refer to our section on closing for more information.

More and more people are buying property "sight unseen" relying on virtual internet tours, photography, map programs and more. We prefer that our clients have visited the property in question. A client we had recently had his heart set on a particular property which seemed like a great deal. Only when we viewed it together in person was he able to get the full effect of the property's location—directly in the flight path—loud and in stereo.

CAN WE GET A VISA EASILY ONCE WE OWN REAL ESTATE IN THE U.S.?

If you invest between $500,000 and $1M, and create jobs, you may be eligible for a Green Card, which means you have the legal right to work and reside in the U.S. as long as you continue to file U.S. income taxes. For all those without that kind of cash to flash, there are a variety of visas that should suit your purposes. Check all the opportunities which may be available to you with an immigration lawyer, to make sure you're making the right choice. If you just use the home as a holiday residence the likelihood is you won't even need a visa for a short term visit of less than 90 days. For visits over 90 days there are myriad visa choices available. Please see the visa section for more info.

CAN WE GET HEALTH INSURANCE IF WE OWN U.S. REAL ESTATE?

Again, depending on how long you intend to stay in the U.S., you may qualify to be covered by travel health insurance from your own country. For longer-term visits/ split residency there are multiple options. Please refer to the health insurance section.

WILL WE HAVE TO PAY TAX IF WE OWN
FLORIDA PROPERTY?

All Florida property owners pay tax based on the assessed value of the property determined by the local municipality. However, the benefits of Florida tax laws far outweigh the negatives in our opinion. There is no sales tax on property purchases, and if you earn money in the state of Florida (for example rental income on an investment property) there is no personal state income tax, which is a huge bonus and incentive for a lot of people choosing to live or buy property here.

Who Pays Real Estate Commissions?

In Florida, real estate sales commissions are paid out of the seller's proceeds. Effectively, this means that Buyers don't incur any cost to have a Realtor working for them. We can't emphasize this concept enough, as the value of working with a Realtor to purchase property is well established in the following sections.

In the Listing Agreement between the Seller and the Listing Broker, one of the provisions specifies the total percentage of commissions to be paid based on the sale price of the property, as well as the commission split between the Listing Broker and Buyer's Broker. In our experience this percentage ranges from 5-7%. The majority of the time the Listing Broker splits the commission 50/50 with the Selling Broker. The Listing Broker, by participating in the MLS system, agrees to pay a percentage of the selling broker's commission.

HOW TO FIND A PROPERTY? GET A REALTOR

Our number one recommendation as you begin your property search? Find the Realtor that is right for you, and you will be immediately putting yourself ahead of the game. Our global clients have great access to the internet and are able to do good research independently. First of all get really clear on what you're looking for and what's most important to you: Is it schools? Beaches? Hospitals? Rentability? Size of the community? Access to cultural amenities? Proximity to a certain airport? Do your research.

Figure out which general geography you want to be in, and then ask friends, family, colleagues, locals, the internet, as many questions as you can to identify which specific locality is going to meet your super-specific needs.

As an added resource to our readers, we offer the **Investments in Florida Realtor Referral Program** as one of the best ways to find a Florida Realtor. These individuals have all been personally pre-assessed by us, show the skill and experience we demand in an agent, and are experts in their region.
www.InvestmentsInFlorida.com

Once you are clear on which area fulfills the most of your wants/needs, research Realtors. The best way is by word of mouth, or by using the **Investments in Florida Realtor Referral Program** at *www.InvestmentsInFlorida.com* to link you with a Realtor that has been qualified by our team. As we keep repeating, finding someone with extensive experience, market knowledge and track record, high level of customer satisfaction, and who has completed many transactions for foreign clients, will be key to your ease and success throughout the entire buying process and beyond. **Take a look at our section on hiring a Realtor for more advice on what questions to ask, what your Realtor should do for you, and how to make sure the person representing you is top notch.**

BACKGROUND RESEARCH

Know your neighbourhood. In our experience, good knowledge of the price history in the specific neighbourhoods you're interested in will help you to have realistic expectations of what you can afford, and this will help you recognize a good deal when it comes along! A good starting point is researching all the homes which recently sold in the area, and getting familiar with why certain properties sold for higher or lower, and which features push the price up. Your agent can give you a Comparative Market Analysis (CMA) which contains all the data, or you can use websites such as Trulia, Zillow, etc. to look it up yourself using the sold listings section.

In general you want to base your research on sold prices, not on the asking price of active listings. In a depreciating market it can sometimes be difficult to get ahead of the price curve, you need your information to be super accurate and up to the minute. In an appreciating market, sellers may get a little aggressive, so that they don't leave money on the table. The goal is to use closed sales figures, and focus on what is of value to you personally, combined with comparable sold data, to figure out the correct price for a property.

A well-versed Realtor should be able to tell you all about price trends in the area you're looking at over both the short and long-term. The area might be experiencing a rise in the market. Or the bubble may have recently burst and prices are on the way down rapidly. Either way, it's important to know the context for your purchase, in order to make a fully informed decision. An experienced agent should know all these details and trends for each micro-market in his or her area. In some cases it's even vital for them to know the difference in price points and trends on a street-by-street basis. A well informed Realtor should know how long the home's been on the market, and how that compares to the general market, and may well be able to find out if there have been previous offers and their reasons for rejection. He or she may even know something of the seller's motivation: if they're desperate to move, or holding out for the full asking price.

NOW BEGINS THE SEARCH IN EARNEST

There are many ways to go about locating your perfect property in the Sunshine state. **Properties in the United States are marketed very differently that in many other countries as they are listed through a service called an MLS or Multiple Listing Service. This is important because it lists every property for sale and disperses the data about each listing across the wide network of agents, brokers and the public it serves.** While public buyers can't access it themselves, once they've hired a Realtor to work for them, information about every property on the market is at their disposal. The listing's data is owned by the real estate broker who has secured the listing agreement with the property owner. Each MLS system (and there are many) enables reciprocal agreements between brokers to be set up, and as much information to be shared about each other's properties as possible. This enables agents and brokers to make commissions on one anothers' listings.

Here are the most common ways international buyers find their properties:

MLS - Multiple Listing Service

A multiple listing service is the most common way for people to find information on all the properties available in their search area. The MLS is an invaluable tool for Realtors in Florida as it contains every property that is listed for sale by a Realtor. The state of Florida is divided into nearly 35 MLS areas, each one being specific and comprehensive to its respective geography. Agents share their listings' information in order to create a comprehensive resource and give the maximum exposure of the property to the maximum number of buyers. **What this means for you, is that once you find the agent that's right to represent you, he or she will have access to this database, and be able to advise and guide you on *any* property that's available in the marketplace.**

It is this transparency of information which sets the Florida MLS system apart from many others in the world. If you, as a buyer, go to three different Realtors' offices with the same search criteria, you would end up with the same results. For example, in our area, if you wanted to live in the master planned neighbourhood called Turtle Rock, all Realtors you consult would have the same six houses for sale, at prices ranging between $350,000 and $680,000. This transparency is clearly a major differentiator, and explains why we place the emphasis on finding the right Realtor. Because the property information is available to everyone, it's the professional you choose to guide you which determines your property buying experience.

All of these transactions then include a reciprocal agreement, so agents earn commission both ways. When you're selling a property, the MLS gives you access to a huge pool of buyers you wouldn't be able to reach otherwise. When you're buying real estate, you have all the listings which fit your property search at your finger tips, and can conduct an in depth search yourself. Many MLS services have additional features such as calculators for real estate taxes, mortgage payments, and utilities, which help you get a clearer financial picture of the real cost of a property.

Our advice is to hire your agent two or three months before you're ready to buy so you can start getting the maximum information on the market. Your agent should begin sending you all the properties which go on the market and are sold in your search area that meet your search criteria, so you have a good and realistic picture of the market. Including what you can really afford and how much your desired features are going to cost you.

Internet Sites - Zillow, Trulia, Realtor.com

The biggest change in the real estate market in recent years has no doubt been the explosion of listing sites such as Zillow, Trulia, ForSaleByOwner.com, Craigslist and Realtor. com. It's now estimated that 60 percent of homebuyers find their property initially through one of these sites, and there is no doubt that access to thousands of properties is of huge benefits to buyers, particularly international buyers looking for real estate in Florida from their home country. These sites are extremely effective in making listings available and putting all the information at the buyers' fingertips. They often include virtual tours, aerial or street views, and many other added features which are enormously helpful.

The role of these internet sites has no doubt changed the role of Realtors going forward. In reality, it makes finding the right Realtor even more important, as you need someone who really adds value. **Now-a-days Realtors' roles are more geared towards providing top quality guidance in how to structure offers, negotiate the many variables with the other party, and step you through the process of inspections, financing, and insurance. In short, they are there to advocate for your interests throughout the**

buying process. You can see that searching out properties for their clients is just the start: the real work begins when you begin thinking about how to structure your offer, get the property under contract, and how to make it to closing.

We frequently encounter situations where clients use the internet to identify the type of home they would like, not knowing anything about the neighborhoods or areas they are searching, to provide the true picture of what they are looking at. While it is extremely helpful for a Realtor to see the types of things that are important to you in a home, the location is just as important. Here is where it is critical to tap into the expertise of a Realtor who has lived and worked there for many years. So that he or she can give you the full context of the living experience in each area, and discuss some of the less tangible quality of life factors, such as distance to shopping and restaurants, proximity to attractions or the beach, and the overall safety of the neighborhood if there are major roads etc. Again and again our clients begin looking in one area through their initial internet search, and then after we are able to educate them fully and take into account their most important home and lifestyle criteria, they end up choosing entirely different areas.

For Sale by Owner (FSBO)

Let's talk about the handful of sellers who may choose to not list their property through the MLS. Their motive usually is that they do not want to pay the broker commission for listing their property in the system. We refer to these as FSBOs. This limits their exposure significantly, but in a market with a large pool of buyers might be viable option. When you, as the buyer, work with a Realtor, a FSBO seller will typically pay a commission to your Realtor.

"Pounding the Pavement"

This is no doubt a time-consuming option, but in our experience buyers have occasionally been able to identify property opportunities ahead of the rest of the market by putting in a huge amount of legwork. This might mean sending a letter to the residents in your chosen neighbourhood asking if anyone is ready to sell, and presenting yourselves as the perfect buyers. Or it might be striking up conversations as you walk by owners, stating your desire to buy in the area, and seeing if they know of anyone thinking about selling. Or it may simply be driving or biking through your chosen area often looking for a For Sale By Owner sign in the garden. Another technique some people use is meeting local agents face to face, and leaving their details and property requirements with them in the hope that should anything which suits their needs come up, the agent may let them know before it hits the MLS or the big property sites, giving them a head start.

It's really important irrespective of whether the right property for you is listed through MLS or comes from a FSBO or by word of mouth, that you share as much info as you possibly can about your wishes, imaginings and desires with your Realtor, so he or she can be on the lookout for the perfect property. Agents who have lived and worked in an area for many years have many relationships and contacts, and you never know when they might have information about things coming on the market through their extensive network.

TYPES OF FLORIDA PROPERTY

The type of property you choose as your future Florida home will be decided by several factors including your personal needs from the property, whether it's intended for financial return or holiday home, your budget, and your knowledge. As the types of property available have different pros and cons, and the descriptions of properties in America may differ from your home country, we think it's useful to outline the most commonly found property types and their benefits for investors.

Oceanfront, Gulf Front and Waterfront Property

Of course, aside from the climate and the sunny reputation, another major draw to Florida as a destination is the waters which surround it, as well as its spectacular lakes, rivers and canals. Among these are over forty waterways designated as outstanding by the Department of Environmental Protection, as well as the U.S.'s premier beach, Siesta Key Beach, in our hometown of Sarasota. Florida's sparkling waters are not only warm, but in most places they are clear and wonderful to swim in.

Those who are in the position to pay the premiums demanded for Oceanfront (Atlantic Ocean side of Florida), Gulf Front (Gulf of Mexico side), beachfront, or waterfront property are well advised to do so. Getting more house for your money off the water may be tempting, but being on the water is the surest way to guarantee you get the most amount of return for your money when re-selling, or in rental income terms. Beachfront property will always be in demand as the sun-seekers, holidaymakers and property buyers flock to beachfront locations to purchase a bit of the Florida good life.

And the waterfront living doesn't begin and end with the beach—much Floridian property is located on canals, rivers, and bays, which offer specific and desirable niche markets for people searching for particular lifestyles: be that fishing, birding, boating, kayaking, or simply being close to the calming properties of the water. These properties each offer different lifestyles for buyers and holidaymakers, and present different niche markets for rental income.

But never fear if waterfront properties are beyond your reach or not the right match, there are still a myriad of property investment opportunities in Florida. From condos, to gated communities, new developments, or golf course living, it all depends on what you want from your money, in terms of both lifestyle and return on investment.

Considerations to remember about waterfront property include that upkeep is significant and a cost to be factored in over and above what it regularly costs to maintain a home. Insurance can also be much higher for properties on the coast.

WATER!! WATER!!! WATER!!!

Commands highest prices both for rental and resale

Most desirable properties in the market generally.

PROS   More in demand

Much more exterior maintenance and costs

Higher insurance

Can be nerve-wracking in storm/flood situations

Maybe safety issues for children

CONS

Single Family

If you can afford to choose a single family home for your property investment or holiday home, you are making a wise use of your money as these homes tend to produce the highest appreciation over time and also the highest rental incomes. The downsides with single family homes include higher cost, higher upkeep costs, and more labour intensive maintenance, especially pool homes. But the rewards are well worth it, especially if you intend to use the home with your family. Note: even if your single family home is not within a Homeowners' Association, there are still likely to be restrictions and rules in place concerning different issues which are often written into the deeds for the home. Your attorney or Realtor should look into these in detail as part of their due diligence on the property on your behalf.

Privacy. Usually good outdoor space
Feeling of own home
Usually more say over the appearance of the property

PROS   Higher desirability for renting

More maintenance than townhouses and condos   CONS
Higher price than townhouses and condos
Higher insurance

Condos

The bread and butter of the Florida property market, condos are a great choice for investors. Not only are they somewhat plentifully available in most of the major areas, they tend to be more affordable, and much easier in terms of upkeep. This is beneficial for international buyers who will only be using the property themselves for part of the year, or not at all. In addition to the perceived ease of ownership, condo living typically affords lower budget accessibility to areas such as beachfront and downtown locations, than the buyer would be able to afford in a single family home. Since condos in the most desirable locations are vertical, the buyer is only paying a fraction of the actual land cost.

Condominiums are usually set up so that each owner owns his or her unit individually, and all the owners in the building have a share of ownership of the common spaces. A board of directors manages the Condominium Association, and this is responsible for the maintenance, upkeep and repair of common areas such as entrances, hallways, stairs and roof.

Condominium associations have very specific rules which govern living in the building. The rules and conditions for owners vary hugely between different Condo Associations. These may include restrictions on pets, or limitations on the size of pets, as well as restrictions on renting out the property. Most condos also have fees which are paid annually for the upkeep of the building and exterior areas, so it's important to factor those into your cost of ownership calculations. It's also important to know all of these things upfront in order to decide if the building you choose is suitable for your lifestyle. Condo Associations have a responsibility to disclose these rules and make the paperwork available to you. For an example of a Condominium Association's rules go to

www.lakesideplaza.com/our-association/governing-documents/rules-and-regulations/

Condos are a great choice to achieve value in the Florida property market also, as return to investment ratio tends to be quite good when renting, and condos are appreciating. The actual amount varies area to area. As mega property portal, Trulia, says: "We recommend condominiums in South Florida in general. The condo market has witnessed as much as a 60 percent increase in selling price, since 2011 and we expect the market to experience a sustained recovery, making now the perfect time to buy."

The condo market seems to be a popular choice with Canadian buyers too, as this recent article in the *Canadian Financial Post* indicates: "About 80 percent of Canadians buying real estate in Florida are purchasing condos. With this product, they can lock the door and walk away and not have to worry about the exterior maintenance."[5]

PROS

Generally very secure

Very minimal maintenance - only the interior

More affordable than townhouses or single family homes

Return rates may still be good despite lower cost

Condo Association handles all maintenance

Unusual to have outdoor space

Neighbour Noise

Little Privacy

Condo Association fees

CONS

Townhouses

Townhouses are properties which tend to be arranged over two or more floors, in areas where ground footprint is at a higher premium. These tend to be good value, as the land value is generally lower than on a similar single-family home which is more spread out. Canadian Real Estate Wealth Magazine reports: "Townhouses are also hot, because they have lower monthly fees than condos but you can typically pick them up for around the same prices. Also, the rents tend to be higher and they attract more family-oriented renters than condos. The areas we recommend our investors purchase in are many of the mid-upper middle class suburbs of Orlando such as Winter Garden, Windermere, Lake Nona and Lake Mary. Vacation rentals are also a very popular option right now for those not as concerned with the short-term return but are looking to win big on the capital gain over the long run."[6]

PROS

Slightly lower heating/cooling bills due to houses on either side.

Less exterior maintenance than single family homes

Usually exterior upkeep managed by HOA

"House" living experience, but usually more affordable than a single family home

Ease of living in a close community - safety and security

You own the land the home sits on as well as the interior and exterior of the home

Often have security

'House' experience but less garden to look after

CONS

Possible neighbour noise

Small gardens or outdoor space

Little say in the exterior look of the property

HOA fees

Sometimes less light than stand alone homes

Less privacy than stand alone homes

Retirement Homes/Villages

Retirement homes and villages are becoming more and more popular as the population ages and more and more baby boomers enter retirement with disposable income and a desire to enjoy their golden years. Retirement villages tend to offer good security, facilities on hand which appeal to seniors, often organized group activities, and social common spaces or entertainment venues. Retirement communities very often have staff on hand, and it may be possible to buy a long-term lease rather than ownership of the entire property, thereby saving you capital but giving you a home of your 'own' for a long time. This may be a simple way of avoiding some of the complications of homeownership.

Safety and security

Help on hand should you need it

Little or no maintenance

PROS   Properties set up for older people

Activities and facilities on site

Fees for extra services

CONS

Homeowners' Associations

It's pertinent to note here that most homes, particularly in upper scale neighbourhoods in Florida, are managed by Homeowners' Associations or HOAs. These differ slightly from the concept of Condominium Associations because the owners of the individual lots do not share ownership of the common areas. These common areas are owned by the HOA itself. Usually they own the title deed, but similar to a Condominium Association, the HOA is responsible for the maintenance and upkeep of the common areas.

Homeowners' Associations are generally responsible for everything that affects the community as a whole, most specifically the exterior appearance of the community. Regulations can manage everything from open house signs, exterior property maintenance, colours you may paint your property, and plants you may use in your garden to what your mailbox looks like, your fencing, and even curtains.

While to many international buyers these restrictions may seem incredibly over-bearing, their purpose is to ensure that the look and feel of the community is maintained and there are myriad benefits to having an HOA manage your community. Specifically, they ensure that property prices are maintained, and no property can be 'letting down the neighbourhood'. To see an example of HOA rules for a neighbourhood, go to *www.bkia.org/images/Documents/2013%20Governing%20Documents.pdf*

Gated Communities

Gated communities are a particularly American phenomenon. They are enclaves of homes—often developed all at the same time with an identical or very similar feel—which have some kind of security or entrance which separates them from the wider community. Gated communities are prized for the security they offer residents, as well as their feeling of community. Often these communities are created around golf courses, so a shared interest brings residents together with other like-minded individuals. They are almost always managed by a HOA.

FORECLOSURES AND SHORT SALES

One of the saddest and most regrettable results of the bursting of the sub-prime mortgage bubble has been the high rate of foreclosures and distressed sales in our state. These statistics are a sad fact of life, and part of the reality that many people were forced to lose their homes. However, we would be remiss in our duties as agents and brokers, if we didn't highlight the investment opportunity presented by these types of sales.

Florida topped the list of states with the highest number of foreclosures in 2012,[7] and while those tangled and difficult cases work their way through the system and may present buyers with headaches, for the tenacious they are an opportunity to achieve good value. Though it's another sad reality, an added effect from the increase in people who no longer own their own homes, is that a larger demand for rentals is created presenting an opportunity for investors looking for return on investment.

David Lockhart, President and CEO of the Federal Reserve Bank of Atlanta, confirmed in 2012, that international buyers are taking note of Florida's foreclosed and short sale market as an investment opportunity, saying: "Our contacts in the real estate sector have noted for some time that international investors, mainly from Canada, Europe and South America, have been active buyers of this area's distressed residential real estate assets."[8]

While the opportunities in this sector are present, and in many instances a great way to achieve value, it is really important to understand the intricacies and the process of a foreclosure or short sale, and to have a really excellent agent representing you who understands fully and completely the tricky nuances of the distressed sale process.

Also something to note: many people seem to think that bank owned and foreclosed homes are often not included in the MLS listings. This is generally not true, most are included, but they may not show up for a while after the lender takes repossession of the home. There is a convoluted process the bank has to go through before they release the property onto the market. This includes allocating an asset manager to be responsible for the property and stabilizing the property so that its value is maintained. Typically this can take up to a few months before the property is listed on the MLS.

SHORT SALES VS. FORECLOSURES

The key difference between short sales and foreclosures is that in a foreclosure the bank takes ownership of the property and forces its sale to recover losses. Whereas a short sale is a delicate negotiation between the property owner and the bank or lender to recover as much as possible from the property's sale to be paid towards the loan owed to the lender.

If you're looking at a property which has been subject to foreclosure or is a short sale, it's important that you understand the process so you know where you stand, how far along the process is, and what your timeframe to ownership might look like.

Process of a Foreclosure

1. **Pre-foreclosure** The lender files an action to the court against the borrower who has failed to keep up their repayments. This includes recording a notice of a pending lawsuit against the borrower. The lender lets the borrower know by mail usually. If there is no response to the court action within the time specified, then the borrower can be found in default. The lender

would then ask the court for a final ruling. If this goes in the lender's favour then the ruling will show the total amount owed to the lender, and the date for the sale of the foreclosed property. The borrower can prevent the foreclosure by paying in full the amount owed to the lender before the date of the foreclosure sale.

2. **Notice of Sale or Auction** The sale date is usually around 30 days after the court ruling is put in place. The notice is published in the local newspaper and the municipal website for a prescribed amount of time, the final notice appearing at least five days before the sale date. The sale is normally held in the county courthouse and/or online. Because of technology it has become easier to buy in this fashion, yet there are cases where there is little or no due diligence period, so this process is only for the savvy buyer who has a team in place to do fast due diligence prior to the sale. We have had clients who have clicked "buy now" and ended up with something which was not what they intended or expected, or worse that had title issues because there were was another lender making claim on the property. The bidder who wins must put down five percent of the property's value as a deposit, with the rest due by the end of the day. If this falls through then a new sale is arranged a minimum of 20 days later. After a successful sale the winner is given the certificate of sale, and the ownership of the property is transferred

within ten days as long as there is no dispute on the sale. The borrower has no way to redeem the property after the certificate of sale is issued.

Process of a Short Sale

In a short sale the local knowledge and experience of your Realtor becomes even more important; in fact it's critical to the success or failure of the deal. Your choice of agent will ultimately determine whether or not you get your home. Your agent needs to have the experience and skill to know exactly the true value of the property, and what it's worth to you. As we reiterated during our presentation in Congress, for our business and any small business with integrity, it's all about the people you have on board and the relationships you build. Nowhere is this more true than in a short sale situation.

SO WHAT IS A SHORT SALE?

A short sale can be defined very simply: where the property sells for less than is owed to the bank. In today's unique real estate environment many buyers are asking for the lender to accept less than is owed and forgive the borrower the difference on the loan. This decision is down to the lender and it requires a lot of paperwork and appraisal to get that decision made. If you're looking to buy a property that is in this process be prepared to wait out the wrangling, and make sure you've got the right agent to help you get your offer accepted.

A Short Sale we listed.....

To illustrate the challenges in dealing with a short sale, we share the story of a property we had listed for two years in a depreciating market. Initially, we had a buyer willing to buy the house for $1.2 million, but the lender was not ready to accept it. Fast forward 15 months and the lender took 280,000 dollars (23 percent) less. Why? In this case the first buyer was ready willing and able, the lender had all of the required info to make a decision, the appraisals supported the offer, but the lender was not ready. 15 months later we worked with a negotiator at the same lender with years of experience who is paid for performance. The difference: We went from contract to closing in 60 days for 280,000 dollars less. Like all things in life, a short sale is all about the people.

OUR ADVICE FOR ANYONE LOOKING AT A SHORT SALE PROPERTY?

1. **Be Patient** Short sales can go through as quickly as 60 days, but more typically take up to six months. The buyer has to be prepared to wait out the process as the bank and the seller hammer out the details of what the lender is prepared to accept.

2. **Get the Right Realtor** Like any real estate deal a short sale is all about the people. Make sure your Realtor has a lot of experience with short sales. An experienced Realtor will keep the deal on track by being persistent and negotiating constantly with the lender or seller's agent. That relationship is absolutely critical to the success of a short sale. Your Realtor also needs to have intimate knowledge of the local market to know the true value of the home.

3. **Don't Count on a Short Sale** The percent of short sales has decreased since 2009/2010. While there are still opportunities, they have become much less prevalent. On one hand that means less "deals" to find, but on the other hand it is a signal that the local real estate and local economies have experienced a solid recovery.

WHERE TO BUY IN FLORIDA?

Florida is world-renowned for some of its treasures. But other gems such as its incredible natural diversity, outstanding beauty, and cultural heritage, go unnoticed by many property hunters drawn to the sun, sea and sand of Florida's traditional hotspots. In fact, we believe that Florida offers an incredible variety to the potential second home owner, a variety which stretches far beyond the glitz and glamour of Miami Beach, or the excitement of the world's largest theme park, which draws 125 million people through its happy gates each year. Beyond this world famous attraction there are 11 National Parks, 1651 places on the National Historic Register, and a UNESCO world heritage site. In addition there are smaller cities with vibrant arts and music scenes, relaxed beach towns, and sleepy backwaters famous for their oysters and seafood, as well as the multicultural living and nightlife of our major metropolises.

There are 700 natural springs (among the largest concentration on earth) offering a myriad of crystal clear waterways for boating, swimming and wildlife viewing opportunities, as well as a verdant mass of waterways across southern Florida, called the Everglades. This habitat once covered 4000 square miles, and is still one of the most diverse ecosystems in North America, and home to alligators, Florida panthers, and hundreds of species of birds. Everglades National Park, the only subtropical preserve in North America, is now a recognized World Heritage Site, an International Biosphere Reserve and a Wetland of International Importance. Add to that 1,200 miles of coastline, boasting some of the best sands in the United States, and mile upon mile of incredible beaches, mangroves, salt marshes, and coral reefs and you have, in our opinion, an incredible amount of diversity, different lifestyle choices and, without a doubt, something to offer every buyer looking for a vacation home or investment.

WHERE TO BUY OVERVIEW

One of the most common requests we get from people searching for Florida real estate is for a general price summary. In other words "where's cheap" to buy. In fact it's really hard to generalize as prices are, like anywhere, affected by myriad nuances in individual markets. Each community can be divided into multiple micro markets, and each micro market has its own sub-market. One example, from our hometown of Sarasota, is Bird Key which is a residential barrier island forming a 500 home micro market. Within that we have three sub-markets: bay front, canal front, and garden homes, each with their own distinct price range.

In an effort to provide some broad strokes to answer this question, however, this very general summary applies:

 Northwest: Prices tend to be lower in the north, which is further from the huge tourist areas and attractions. This may not be the best investment for a rental return, but as a holiday home and lifestyle choice it is still a splendid place to buy, and a winner for those seeking a quieter, gentler pace of life.

 Southeast: As another sweeping generalization, the south east Atlantic coast—encompassing Miami, Ft Lauderdale, and Palm Beach up to Orlando—tends to be generally pricier than the south-western Gulf coast. This stretch includes some of the priciest residences in America, with multi-million dollar homes pushing up the median house prices. However, if you choose your area wisely, away from the ultra-rich enclaves of Palm Beach, it's still possible to get a three bedroom, single family home with a pool for around the $250,000 mark. In the south Florida market returns are less, ranging from 6–10 per cent, but appreciation and prices are much greater. However, it depends on the investor's appetite for risk and investment goals.[9]

The Miami property market is really a law unto itself. Typical apartment prices begin around $300,000—which isn't necessarily expensive to be in one of the most happening metropolises in the world and with all that the city has to offer. In fact, Miami is perhaps the one location which has bounced back the fastest, with an influx of buyers from Latin America. Inventory is now fairly low, which means prices are only going one way. However it's still possible to get deals on condos, as this market experienced a construction boom and so has the most inventory available.

 Northeast/Central: The big attractions of Disney, Universal and Sea World are concentrated around the centre of the state, and we think the massive tourism potential of these areas does keep prices high—but also offers a huge potential for returns from tourism rentals, so values are probably fair. According to Shalimar Santiago, CEO of Investors Adviser's Network, central Florida is currently the hottest market, from Orlando to the Tampa region, with returns yielding on average 8–12 per cent.[10]

 Southwest: Prices are somewhat lower than the southeast. Strong rental potential in the summer comes from Europeans and Americans in school summer holidays. In terms of lifestyle, this coastline is fabulous, and boasts some of the best beaches in the country. This has helped to skyrocket the waterfront property prices—which can be more than double the price of comparable properties in the Orlando area, and helps explain why 60 percent of the wealthiest people in the country winter either on this southwestern Gulf coast in Naples, or at Palm Beach on the south east Atlantic coast.

Our purpose is not to be a travel book. It is to provide an overview of the four primary areas of Florida so that you can understand the lifestyle of these areas, to lay a foundation of the considerations when purchasing property in Florida. And perhaps, most importantly, to match you with people to work with during the researching, viewing and buying process, so that you can find that great place.

Market Summaries

Southeast Quadrant

West Palm Beach

Population: 101,000

Condo: $100,000 - $3M

Family Home: $150,000 - $3.9M

Waterfront: (Palm Beach): $150,000 - $59M

Investment Potential Rating: ****

Nearest International Airport: Palm Beach
International Airport

West Palm Beach is a thriving and busy city with plenty of diversity and a vibrant culture. Set along the Intracoastal Waterway, it has an historic downtown, as well as many other historic areas. West Palm Beach is a centre for the arts and history with the acclaimed Antique Row, the Kravis Center for the Performing Arts, and the Norton Art Museum. There are two important shopping areas centred on Clematis Street and City Place, which have great shops, restaurants and nightlife. West Palm Beach has a tropical rainforest climate, and is one of the wetter cities in the U.S.

The West Palm Beach real estate market is a complex one, and over the last year has experienced a 44 percent drop in inventory and 28 percent rise in median price,[11] all of which creates an incredibly tight and competitive market. However, property here is a safe long term bet. In West Palm Beach the waterfront market is primarily made up of waterfront condos—many of which are listed as single family homes. It's possible to snap up a water view one bedroom condo for $150,000, and at the top end of the market stunning luxury condos with three bedrooms and water views are available from around $800,000 to $3 million. Off the water it's possible to get a three bedroom, new build golf course home for $150,000, or a comfortable lake view home for around $200,000. And there are beautiful five bedroom pool homes in the $500,000 range. Heading across to Palm Beach itself, you will discover some of the most expensive property in America, with beach front estates quite regularly selling for tens of millions, the most expensive currently listed? An eye-watering $59 million dollars.

Boca Raton

Population: 84,000

Condo: $123,000 - $7.9M

Family Home: $500,000 - $11.9M

Waterfront: $400,000 - $11.9M

Investment Potential Rating: ***

Nearest International Airport: Fort Lauderdale-Hollywood International Airport, 19.45 miles

Boca Raton lies in the heart of Florida's Gold Coast and in Palm Beach county. It has something to suit everyone looking for the resort lifestyle, fine restaurants, world class golf courses, and great beaches. In addition, high end shopping boutiques, excellent museums and specialty shops can be found all over the city. This is truly gated community heaven, with three of the most expensive gated communities in the U.S. located in the city. Created in large part by Addison Mizner in the early part of the 20th Century, the city was planned from the outset as a playground for the rich and the fabulous, and has largely succeeded in fulfilling its aim. It boasts 44 parks, and 20 golf courses. Wealth abounds, and beautiful property and communities surround the water, the golf courses and the downtown areas.

Again, in Boca Raton the real estate market revolves around the condo market. It's possible to get a simple pool resort condo for around $120,000, but really for a decent family condo close to the beach you would need to spend at least $300,000 and for ocean views at least $380,000. There is a lot more choice for waterfront condos in the $500,000 upwards range. There aren't really many single family homes in Boca Raton under $500,000—this is a competitive and expensive market and those on budgets under half a million would be almost certainly confined to the condo market. Beachfront homes are obviously only available in the upper reaches of $6 million or so plus.

Port St. Lucie

Population: 155,000

Condo: $70,000 - $330,000

Family Home: $100,000 - $1.9M

Waterfront: $170,000 - $1.9M

Investment Potential Rating: ****

Nearest International Airport: Palm Beach
International Airport - 53 miles

Lying on Florida's Treasure Coast and within an hour's drive of Palm Beach, Port St. Lucie is a less developed, and more traditional Florida City. Prices here are lower than in wealthier parts of the region, and the city is growing and thriving, making it a good choice for those willing to go the extra mile to get good value and lifestyle. The surrounding countryside is lovely with environmental preserves to hike, rivers to kayak, and horse riding on nearby beaches.

Prices are a big incentive in Port St. Lucie. Investors can buy a condo for $65,000 -$70,000 and rent it out long-term for $850/month. This is a good return, and it is difficult to find this purchase price with a 6-7 percent return in other Florida cities. Port St. Lucie is lesser known than other cities on this coast, but those looking for a great long term investment would be wise to consider it. This community is not the right one if you're looking for a holiday home or a place you can rent out as a short vacation rental investment. It's possible to get a three bedroom condo here for around

$80,000 and a decent water view condo for around $160,000. The entry point for single family homes can be as low as $100,000. Spacious waterfront homes with private dock are available from around the $650,000 mark. At the top end of the market in the $1.2m to $1.9m range there are some wonderful homes which offer incredible lifestyle, at a price point lower than in towns such as Ft Lauderdale, Orlando, or West Palm Beach.

Ft. Lauderdale

Population: 165,000
Condo: $150,000 - $14M
Family Home: $300,000 - $32M
Waterfront: $400,000 - $32M
Investment Potential Rating: ***
Nearest International Airport: Fort Lauderdale Hollywood International Airport, 5 miles.

Fort Lauderdale made its name back in the day as a spring break destination, but the city nowadays has a far more glamorous image. On its bustling streets the rich and famous go about their business, and beachfront mansions, as well as historic neighbourhoods with tree-lined streets, help make the property market expensive. The city is known for its shopping, its beaches and its yachting scene, sometimes being referred to as a mega-yacht capital. The 165 miles of canals, and access to the Intracoastal waterway make it a popular destination for boaters of all shapes and sizes. As well as this, there is a thriving arts scene, performing arts centre, and museums. The Everglades are close by for natural pleasures and the Atlantic Ocean provides water activities in abundance. People choose Fort Lauderdale as a quieter location than Miami, but still with the diverse and sophisticated nightlife, and shopping scene which that city is famous for.

The Fort Lauderdale market is popular with Canadian buyers, many of whom are buying condos which need work, and renovating them to sell for profit. High net worth Europeans are still buying desirable South Beach property, although there has been less activity from Germany, Italy and Britain in the last few years due to the economy there. The market in Fort Lauderdale has recovered well, with steadily rising prices, and a fairly healthy eight months of inventory in the market. Although that inventory level is 33 percent down from the same time last year. The high end of the market is thriving in Fort Lauderdale, with a large number of properties over the $2 million mark, and many over $10 million. At the very top end, mansions on the water can set you back as much as $32 million. For more modest price points such as entry level properties suitable for refurbishment, there really isn't much inventory below $150,000. And at that price point the home would be for long-term rental or long-term appreciation, rather than the vacation rental market. At $250,000 it's possible to get a two bedroom townhouse which might suit as a vacation home, but for a modest water view three bedroom single family home, you're really looking at $500,000 upwards. In the condo market it's possible to get a one bedroom condo a couple blocks from the beach, requiring refurbishment, for around $150,000. Otherwise a waterfront two bedroom condo on the Intracoastal Waterway water front will set you back $400,000 or more. At the luxury end of the condo market there is a sprinkling of properties which reach the $14 million mark, but most of the luxury family condo market lies in the $1 million to $3 million range.

Miami

Population: 413,000
Condo: $300,000-$27M
Family Home: $300,000 - $25M
Waterfront: $600,000 - $25M
Investment Potential Rating: ****
Nearest International Airport: Miami International Airport

The Miami property market could really fill an entire book itself. The vast metropolis has pretty much everything to offer buyers from sprawling residential areas, to vast oceanfront mansions, to uber-hip city apartments. Miami also ranks as a professional sports hub, with one American football team, one baseball team, one hockey team, and one basketball team. It's also known as a destination for the arts, and has several major concert venues.

The Miami property market fared badly during the crash, with prices falling low and hard. However it has bounced back with a vengeance, and now seems to be on a much firmer footing as a world-class destination with an urban, hip vibe similar to Barcelona, Istanbul, or Medellin. Miami saw an explosion of foreign investment at its lowest point, which did help to re-invigorate and recover the market. Now as prices have risen the bargain-hunter money is looking elsewhere, and Miami prices are tighter, with little opportunity left. The better opportunities require greater patience and resolve to find.

This market, according to our colleagues, is seeing shortage of properties for sale and rising prices, though huge new construction is under way. Miami has always been a very multi cultural city, and has huge South American communities. In recent years this has included large influxes of international buyers from Brazil and Venezuela. The city's nightclubs, celebrities, party scene, art scene and yachting scene are world-renowned. Add to that, cutting-edge restaurants, a thriving economy, and some of the liveliest city beaches in the world, and you have the heady mix which is Miami.

Inventory under $200k is 60 percent less now than it was in 2012. Really to get into this market buyers need to be willing to spend at least $300k. At the top end of the market condos on the waterfront in the hottest neighbourhoods fetch up to a staggering $27 million, while there are stunning single family homes available waterfront for $20 million. If you're looking for beachfront luxury, you can snap up a condo on Fisher Island for $11 million or so. At the lower price points, $300,000 will get you a one bedroom apartment in a desirable neighbourhood in the heart of the city, or a three bedroom home in a managed community away from the buzz of the centre. There are well appointed single family pool homes available for around $600,000 though if you want to be where the action is, the same price will get you a one bedroom luxury waterfront condo. At the $1 million mark there are five bed lakefront homes available, otherwise, if you want to be waterfront in a single family home you're looking at spending at the very least $3.5 million. Miami is a super competitive market, but also a sound long-term investment if you can get in. Again, it all comes back to whether you want a vacation home, or a long-term rental and what kind of return you're looking for. Either way, make no mistake, the Miami market is hot.

Southwest Quadrant

Tampa

Population: 335,000

Condos: $50,000 - $1.2M

Family Home: $175,000 - $3M

Waterfront: $200,000 - $5M

Investment Potential Rating: ***

Nearest International Airport: Tampa International Airport

Tampa is the third largest city in Florida and has all the attractions and amenities you would expect in a big city with a rich history: an excellent museum, aquarium, theatre and zoo, as well as being home to Busch Gardens, and Tampa International Airport, which makes it a convenient entry point for visitors, and a tourism destination in its own right. In the surrounding areas there are lots of opportunities for golfing, water sports and biking, making Tampa a very desirable location.

The Tampa investment market of late has been fairly aggressive, with large investors buying up huge swathes of homes and land, particularly foreclosed homes. However there is still inventory in the market, and as of July 2013 inventory grew by 11 percent which is a good indicator there is some choice in the market although inventory is decreasing slowly long-term. Also noteworthy: the median asking price increased by 6.5 percent on the previous month[12] to $189,000. These numbers are consistent with the general pattern in the market, which is consistent inventory, and steadily rising prices. The median asking price peaked in April 2006, and is now 34.3 percent lower than that price, but has still risen by more than a third from its lowest ever point in 2011. This provides solid information that the market is steadily appreciating.

St. Petersburg

Population: 244,000
Condo: $65,000 - $1M
Family Home: $150,000 - $2M
Waterfront: $100,000 - $7M
Investment Potential Rating: ****
Nearest International Airport - Tampa International Airport: 15 miles, Sarasota - Bradenton International Airport - 26 miles.

St. Petersburg is a popular holiday destination and the second largest city in the Tampa Bay area. The city is nicknamed "The Sunshine City" as it reportedly enjoys 361 days of sunshine a year. In 2011 American Style magazine ranked St. Petersburg as America's number one mid-size city, due in part to its vibrant arts scene. The city has a subtropical climate, with a definite rainy season from June through to September, though many different micro climates exist along its shores due to its peninsula location and the shape of its bay. St. Petersburg is famous for its Salvador Dali museum, as well as its children's museum, and Museum of Fine Arts. For those seeking natural splendour, Boyd Hill Nature Park on the shores of Lake Maggiore, is a 245-acre preserve home to many of Tampa Bay's rare wildlife and endangered plants.

St. Petersburg is popular with Europeans looking for Florida real estate as the downtown feels like a little French Riviera. Often they are looking to refurbish a property and sell it at a profit, and many are looking for a 15 percent return on their investment. While there aren't direct international flights—and this may put some people off initially—once most do the trip once or twice, they realize how accessible the city and how easy the transfer is. You may also be getting better value due to the lack of direct international flights. The median asking price in St. Petersburg is currently $129,000, which is up 13 percent on a year ago, and inventory is at only 1,564 properties which is incredibly low for a county this size. This is about the standard amount of inventory for the last couple years, and indicates there is fierce competition, particularly at the lower end of the market. Our Realtors in the field there indicate that these properties sell as soon as they hit the market. Prices are on the rise, so if you can get a property now, you are likely making a good investment.

Sarasota

Population: 51,000

Condo: $100,000 - $4M

Family Home: $200,000 - $10M

Waterfront: $250,000 - $10M

Investment Potential Rating: ****

Nearest Intl Airport: Sarasota-Bradenton Intl Airport - 5 miles.

Sarasota not only sits along the Gulf of Mexico, but also includes seven barrier islands. The result is a panoramic landscape of several distinct beaches, bay estuaries, bridges, and countless canals, bayous and smaller waterways that pervade many neighborhoods. Each island (also referred to as a Key) offers its own lifestyle and identity. Sarasota's legacy is deeply tied to the circus magnate, John Ringling. Ringling made Sarasota his winter home and did much to transform its development. With him he also brought his wealthy peers from the mid-western United States, who in turn created a legacy of philanthropy. The result is that today Sarasota has a vibrant culture of the arts, with its own opera, ballet, and one of the most prolific and profitable performing arts centres in the country. Siesta Key Beach, on one of Sarasota's barrier islands, is ranked as the #1 beach in the U.S., and Sarasota itself is known as one of the top retirement destinations in America. Add to that the abundant flora and fauna of Sarasota's waterways, Myakka state park, good schools and low crime, and you have a great lifestyle destination. If you were to aggregate all of the public land available for walking, biking and trekking, Sarasota County it would be the 23rd largest national park in the United States. With its beautiful sunsets, white sandy beaches, and vibrant arts community, Sarasota has experienced an upsurge in international holidaymakers and investors.

Our team of Sarasota Realtors has over 50 years combined experience in this area. Of course we're biased, as Lee grew up along this beautiful waterfront and we have chosen to raise our kids here. But putting on our Duke MBA hats, we also know firsthand what a great investment Sarasota can be—especially in the high end and luxury waterfront markets, where properties generally outperform the middle and lower ends of the market. More than that, we believe Sarasota offers an exceptional lifestyle choice, and is growing in popularity each day, for exactly that reason.

Since the pendulum swung back in mid 2013 creating a sellers' market, Sarasota is settling in to a more balanced market where the buyers and sellers are now on more equal footing. There is healthy competition in the market for the best properties. Prices are rising, and the right property bought now will likely continue to appreciate. As has held true in recent years, at the higher end of the market there are some great opportunities to be had, as the most competition is for properties between $100,000 and $750,000, where 80 percent of the market lies.

Ft. Myers

Population: 62,000

Condo: $100,000 - $2.4M

Family Home: $250,000　$14M

Waterfront: $500,000 - $14M

Investment Potential Rating: ***

Nearest Intl Airport: Southwest Florida Intl

Airport - 14 miles.

Fort Myers is a smallish city that forms the gateway to Florida's south west, and primary tourism destinations. The city has year round warm weather, as its climate lies on the cusp between tropical and sub-tropical. As with much of Florida, the warm winters make it popular for snowbirds (people looking to escape cold winters). Indeed, two of the city's most famous residents, Thomas Edison and Henry Ford, famously were doing just that when they chose Fort Myers to build their beautiful estates, which are now tourist attractions. Fort Myers is popular for its fishing, beaches and shopping, with an historic downtown. The city also benefits from having South West Florida International Airport 10 miles away, and for international buyers this is a bonus as it's served by many direct flights from Europe.

Fort Myers is a very popular market for Europeans, with some Realtors reporting that European clients make up 80 percent of their business. There are flights to Fort Myers from Dusseldorf, which creates a popular route for many

Europeans who choose to connect from their home city, through Dusseldorf, direct to Florida. The median home price in Fort Myers is now at $189,000 which is a seven percent increase on a year ago,[13] and inventory has decreased by 18 percent in the same period. This indicates that inventory is low, and it's a competitive market, but prices aren't perhaps rising as fast as in some of the other Florida markets. However, that's not necessarily a bad thing: steady and healthy appreciation is always indicative of a stable market.

Cape Coral

Population: 154,000
Condo: $80,000 - $380,000
Family Home: $160,000 - $5M
Waterfront: $500,000 - $5M
Investment Potential Rating: ***
Nearest Intl Airport: Southwest Florida Intl
Airport - 14 miles.

Not far from Fort Myers lies Cape Coral, another popular international property investment destination. Cape Coral was founded in 1957 and was a completely pre-planned city which makes it unusual. It's the largest city between Tampa and Miami and is referred to as a 'waterfront wonderland' as it has over 400 miles of waterways. In fact, Cape Coral is the city with the largest number of canals in the world. This makes it a great investment destination for those who enjoy canal side living, fishing and wildlife. Cape Coral's golf courses, and Gulf Coast beaches are also a major draw and the city also has a popular water park. Since the 1990s Cape Coral has attracted a younger crowd and more families, as employment opportunities have increased. Twenty percent of the population is also seasonal, which points to a good retirement, holiday and tourism investment potential. The summers in Cape Coral are very warm, humid and rainy, while the winters are dry with moderate temperatures.

Cape Coral experienced a nearly 40 percent drop in its median house price at the lowest point during the recession. However, while not back up to those heady bubble heights, the market has recovered steadily, with the median house price now reaching $200,000, a 14 percent increase on the previous year.[14] Inventory is steadily decreasing as well, all good signs of a market on the up and investment potential.

Naples

Population: 19,000
Condo: $200,000 - $6M
Family Home: $300,000 - $20M
Waterfront: $2M - $20M
Investment Potential Rating: ***
Nearest Intl Airport: Southwest Florida International Airport, 26miles, Naples Municipal Airport, 2 miles

Naples is one of the higher end resort destinations on Florida's southwestern coast. The city sits on the Gulf of Mexico and enjoys cool ocean breezes and beautiful beaches, which have helped make it one of America's most popular resort destinations for rich and famous holiday makers. Naples has some world-class shopping on stylish Fifth Avenue in its historic downtown, and many wonderful waterfront restaurants and glamorous bars, beach clubs and hotels. Naples also boasts plenty of art galleries, chic boutiques and theatre to keep visitors entertained. It is an attractive city, with lots of green areas, and a sidewalk cafe culture which helps it draw a European crowd. It also has a thriving arts and cultural scene whether it be philharmonic, Broadway or entertainment. Throughout the year there are many seafood fairs, art exhibitions and concerts in the afternoon. For outdoor pursuits Naples boasts 12 golf courses in the Naples/Bonita springs area, and huge planned golf communities which offer tropical lifestyle even during the winter months. Naples also appeals to many Europeans and Canadians due to its proximity to the beach, and with less traffic that the east coast of Florida, as well as direct European flights.

Inventory in Naples has decreased significantly in the last year, at least by 18 percent, and sales continue to be high, amounting to less than six months of inventory. Median house prices have increased by 13 percent on the previous year, rising to $220,000.[15] Naples has investment properties available in the $100-250,000 and $600,000-2M regions, but is particularly low on inventory in the middle brackets. Overall, there isn't much inventory under $300,000. However there is lots of new building in Naples, partly to try and meet the inventory demand, and buyers pay a premium for these favoured new builds.

Northwest Quadrant

Although it is a less famous part of Florida, the northwest has many wonderful attributes to recommend. Sometimes known as the Panhandle, this stretch of the coastline is less developed than the areas on the southern peninsula. The northwestern coastline, otherwise known as the 'Emerald Coast', has some of the most unspoiled beaches in the State, and is highly regarded for its chilled, outdoorsy vibe.

This area is some of the hilliest of Florida's landscape, and also has some of the state's most amazing natural attractions. These include many caverns, the majority of the State's natural springs, and abundant, pristine, white quartz beaches. This part of Florida is definitely hotter than southern parts of the state, with long summers, and mild winters, and occasionally temperatures over 100 degrees fahrenheit. The state capital in Tallahassee is a centre for trade and agriculture, and is recognized as a tech centre for industry in the state with many multi-nationals having their headquarters there.

Tallahassee (state capital)

Population: 180,000
Condo: $90,000 - $290,000
Family Home: $120,000 - $3.9M
Waterfront : N/A
Investment Potential Rating: **
Nearest International Airport: Tallahassee Regional Airport

Tallahassee is a genteel city lying in the Red Hills bio-region of the panhandle. Its southern roots are evidenced everywhere in its architecture and pace of life. The city lies in one of the most bio-diverse regions of the U.S. and is regarded by the nature conservancy as one of America's "last great places". The city is culturally diverse with Greek, Asian and Celtic heritage. Tallahassee is a historically important city with significant roles in Southern history, and the museum and arts districts reflect this, with many cultural events, festivals and historical learning opportunities.

The city is not renowned as a tourism destination, and for that reason, it may not be the best investment if you're looking to use your property as a holiday home and rent it the rest of the time. However, if you're looking for a property to rent out for a long term rental income, there are some good deals to be had. With a $120,000 property renting for around $1,300 per month,[16] investment buyers can hope to achieve returns of between seven and eight percent. Entry point to the market is lower than in some more touristy parts of Florida, with median price hovering around $140,000 and very little inventory at the higher end of the market over a million. Total inventory is at about nine months, which is fairly healthy and not too competitive—indicating there is choice for buyers in the market. Inventory has increased over the last 12 months, indicating properties aren't moving swiftly off the market, although sales are up on last year.

Panama City

Population: 36,000
Condo: $70,000- $1.4M
Family Home: $100,000 - $3.5M
Waterfront: N/A
Investment Potential Rating: ***
Nearest International Airport: Northwest Florida Beaches International Airport, 22 miles.

Another northwestern gem, Panama City has access to some beautiful beaches, as well as the many water sports, and activities this stretch of the Gulf Coast provides. This area is a favourite destination for families, offering both wonderful beaches and wildlife, and easy access to amusement parks, golf courses and entertainment. Here the market is looking fairly healthy, with prices rising steadily. Although the condo market has been over supplied in recent years, it now looks like inventory is being absorbed by the market. In fact, in the first quarter of 2013 inventory decreased by 36 percent on the same period in 2012. In addition sales were up by 23 percent, indicating the market is on the rise and healthier than it has been in the last few years.[17]

Pensacola

Population: 51,000
Condo: $62,000 - $1.2M
Family Home: $160,000 - $3.5M
Waterfront: $265,000 - $3.5M
Investment Potential Rating: ***
Nearest International Airport: Pensacola International Airport, 2 miles.

Pensacola is an historic Florida town, with a thriving arts scene and some great entertainment. There is a great aviation museum, pre-civil war fortresses, history museums, water parks, the National Naval Museum, and a delightful historic downtown with views of Pensacola Bay, where you can dine at one of the town's many and varied restaurants. Pensacola has a variety of arts and cultural festivals throughout the year including a well-known Mardi Gras celebration. Add to that 52 miles of coastline, rivers and the Gulf of Mexico— where you can spot dolphins, go deep sea fishing, or join the kayakers in the canoe capital of Florida—and it's clear Pensacola has something for everyone.

The Pensacola real estate market has been on the up in recent times along with most of the rest of Florida. Incredibly, we found waterfront single family homes there for around the $265,000 mark, and waterfront condos at $150,000. Condos in pool complexes were available for around $62,000, all of which make this an affordable entry point market, and one in which you certainly get bang for your buck. At the top end of the market, there are a handful of homes over the $2 million mark, and some really great waterfront homes in the $450,000 to $1.7 million band. There is a good amount of inventory, but it is moving, and sales are up 17 percent on the same period last year. Median sale price has crept above the $160,000 mark, but there are still some great deals to be had.

Northeast/Central Quadrant

Jacksonville

Population: 827,908 (Jacksonville Beach 21,000)

Condo: $70,000- $1.9M

Family Home: $180,000 - $5.9M

Waterfront : $460,000 - $5.9M

Investment Potential Rating: ***

Nearest International Airport: Jacksonville International Airport, 10 miles from Jacksonville, 28 miles from Jacksonville Beach.

Jacksonville is the largest city in Florida by population, and the largest city in the U.S. by area. It's an historic, sprawling city, and Florida's largest seaport—featured as a key supply point in the Civil War. The city has a thriving economy with banking, insurance, healthcare, and tourism forming its key industries. Tourism, particularly surrounding golf, is an important focus and there are many excellent golf courses. The city boasts an historic movie palace, an excellent theatre, a centre for the performing arts, and a zoo. The music scene is of particular note with a symphony orchestra, a large arena which attracts national acts, and a thriving jazz culture. There is a yearly jazz festival and Ray Charles played regularly in Jacksonville before he discovered fame and fortune.

Jacksonville Beach is a beach and resort community sitting on the coast just outside Jacksonville. It forms part of the Jacksonville coastal communities that include Mayport, Atlantic Beach, Neptune Beach and Ponte Vedra Beach. These communities are a convenient distance from the city, but offer excellent beach lifestyle opportunities and the facilities one would expect in small resort towns.

The Jacksonville real estate market is ripe for investment now, as is true of most of Florida. Inventory is down almost 30 percent on this time last year, and median home price has increased by 6.8 percent in the same time frame. There are now just four months of inventory in the market—so there is some competition—but also some good values to be achieved in terms of lifestyle. If you are looking for a pool complex condo you can find them from around $90,000 up, with some lovely luxury condos available from $180,000 onwards.

Jacksonville has a healthy luxury market, with a fair bit of inventory over the $2 million mark, and some incredible value properties lying in the $750,000 to $1.5 million bracket. We found waterfront family homes starting from around $460,000 and luxury waterfront condos starting at around $325,000. Most of the waterfront in Jacksonville itself is situated on the St John's River body of water, with more waterfront property situated on the actual beach at Jacksonville Beach. This is a smaller community, with much less inventory. Here, condos with water views start around

$180,000 and waterfront homes range from about $500,000 to $2.3 million.

Gainesville

Population: 124,000
Condo: $55,000 - $220,000
Family Home: $180,000 - $2.4M
Waterfront: N/A
Investment Potential Rating: ***
Nearest International Airport: Jacksonville International Airport, 80 miles.

Gainesville is a medium sized city right in the middle of the northern part of Florida. The city's location is convenient for both the coasts, and also Orlando and Tampa, which are a 90 minute and two hour drive away, respectively. The city has a fascinating southern heritage and Civil War history. Downtown has many beautiful historic buildings including the famous Hippodrome State Theatre. There are several good historical museums, a butterfly rainforest, a railroad museum, and a museum of art, as well as an historic state park and a good reparatory theatre.

The city is dominated by the University of Florida campus, which may offer consistent rental income potential for investors. In 2007 Gainesville was voted number one place to live in North America. Gainesville is also known as "Tree City USA" in reference to the wide variety of tree species, and dense tree canopies belonging to the city. Gainesville is also surrounded by easily accessible state parks and is close to Newman's Lake. The climate is humid subtropical, but with greater weather variation over the year than other areas of the state, and varied flora and fauna also in comparison to the coastal regions of Florida.

Gainesville has a wide variety of family homes available and a fairly limited condo market. At the top end of the market there are luxury homes above $2 M. There are some really spacious and desirable new build four bedroom family homes in the $285,000 bracket. The market is picking up, with the number of sales by the middle of 2013 jumping fifty percent on the previous year. Home prices are climbing, but somewhat more slowly than in other Florida cities, rising only 4.7 percent since the same period in 2012. But hey, a rise is still good, slow and steady may well win the race when it comes to Florida property. Investment homes for the University rental market are recommended here as a good long-term investment.

Daytona Beach

Population: 61,000

Condo: $60,000 - $1.4M

Family Home: $160,000 - $7.7M

Waterfront: $400,000 - $7.7M

Investment Potential Rating: ****

Nearest International Airport: Daytona Beach International Airport, 3 Miles

Daytona Beach is sometimes called the most famous beach town in America, and is also a mecca for motor sports, being the location of the Daytona International Speedway and the headquarters of NASCAR. The city has a variety of historic districts, a water park, a museum of arts and sciences, a museum of photography, and the ocean centre. Massive groups of out-of-towners arriving for various events throughout the calendar can swell population to over 200,000. There is the wide range of activities, shopping and nightlife you would expect to cater to huge groups of tourists, and 23 miles of beaches to be enjoyed in the Daytona Beach area. There are also a wide range of cultural activities, including international music festivals, and many art galleries and museums.

Daytona Beach has a thriving condo market with 'condotels' available waterfront for around a $60,000 starting price. These are investment properties, in essence, a studio hotel room with mini kitchen, catering directly to the seasonal rental market. Waterfront family condos can be found from around $140,000 and family homes a block from the water start at around $240,000. Beachfront properties can be found for $400,000 rising to the top price of $7.7 million, although most of the luxury market in fact lies in the $750,000 to $2.4 million range. Inventory is around 30 percent down on the same time last year, and prices are rising steadily.

St. Augustine

Population: 13,000

Condo: $60,000 - $700,000

Family Home: $140,000 - $3.9M

Waterfront: $240,000 - $3.9M

Investment Potential Rating: **

Nearest International Airport: Jacksonville International Airport, 28 miles.

St. Augustine is the longest continually inhabited European-founded city in America, and was the Spanish capital of Florida for 200 years. As a result it has a rich colonial, post-colonial, and civil war history which is still in evidence today. The many museums, landmarks and architecture reflect the Greek, Spanish, English, Native American and African American heritage of the city. St. Augustine played a significant part in the Civil Rights movement, and there are many monuments and museums throughout the city marking the story of its recent past. St. Augustine is a relatively small city, which means the surrounding beaches are quiet and relatively unspoiled, and its rich past makes for a charming holiday experience, attracting large numbers of tourists. There are further attractions including an alligator farm, Anastasia State Park, and the World Golf hall of fame.

St. Augustine is popular with international investors, including Spanish, Portuguese and Latin American buyers. Many foreigners are also sending their children to boarding school here in the hope of them getting into American colleges. The St. Augustine market is showing a steady recovery, and with around five months of inventory, competition will be heating up. The average sale price is up 10 percent on last year, and prices are rising steadily. There are still great values out there in St. Augustine. At the top end of the market there are a handful of properties fetching prices over $2 million, while in the upper regions of $600,000 to $800,000 there are some beautiful beachfront single family homes available. Buyers can buy a three bedroom single family with direct beach access for around the $500,000 mark, or two bedroom ocean view townhouses—a stone's throw from the sand—start at an affordable $240,000. Away from the water it's possible to get a four bedroom pool home for around $220,000. Decent condos are available in beachfront developments starting at $110,000 for a one bedroom. Elsewhere, off the water, condos can be snapped up from around $60,000 in nice developments. The condo market doesn't have a huge amount of inventory, and there isn't much choice for super luxurious top end condos, the most expensive are around $700,000 in St. Augustine.

Ocala

Population: 56,000

Condo: $45,000 - $321,000

Family Home: $120,000 - $12 M

Waterfront: N/A

Investment Potential Rating: ***

Nearest International Airport: Ocala International Airport. (Private) Orlando International Airport, 90 miles.

Ocala is a small city, which is famous as 'horse capital of the world' being one of the foremost areas in the world for the breeding and training of racehorses. It is an area that experienced massive growth in the late 20th century due to the arrival of Disney World seventy miles away, and the increasing popularity of the area as a retirement destination. The town has an historic district, and boasts a good symphony orchestra and a civic theatre. Ocala has a very distinct two seasons to its year, with a very hot dry season and a cool rainy season. The city is also famous for its Kentucky bluegrass terrain, as well as the largest artesian spring formation in the world, and the second largest national forest in Florida.

If you're looking for investment property then Ocala is a good choice for long-term investment, rather that short-term holiday rentals, as there isn't much of a tourist turnover in the city itself. Super-affordable entry points such as $45,000 for a golf course view condo, and $120,000 for a new build—very rentable—three bedroom family home, make this a good choice for those with lower budgets. At the top end of the market $12 million will get you a spectacular family home, but may not be the most practical investment for international buyers, as the 300 acres which comes along with it may be challenging to manage from abroad. What you do definitely get in Ocala is bang for your buck when it comes to acreage. Although this may not be a primary motivator for foreign buyers, it's worth noting that even in the $240,000 range you're looking at farms, ranches and elegant family homes with at least two or three acres. The market is improving, though it has experienced a slower recovery than other parts of Florida. But in May and June of 2013 sales were over 25 percent higher than 2012 and inventory was 17 percent down.

Orlando

Population: 238,000

Condo: $100,000 - $2.5M

Family Home: $200,000 - $15M

Waterfront: N/A

Investment Potential Rating: ***

Nearest International Airport: Orlando International Airport.

Orlando is of course first and foremost known for its proximity to Disneyworld, which lies 24 miles away from its downtown. It is nicknamed "The City Beautiful" and has many other great attractions to recommend it, but it's for its theme parks that it's truly well known. Other parks situated in Orlando include Sea World, Universal Studios, and Wet n' Wild, as well as many others. These huge tourism attractions help it regularly rank as the most visited city in America.

The downtown area of the city is centered around the historic district, with the city's symbolic fountain at Lake Eola forming the focal point. Some world class shopping is to be found in Orlando, and it is a centre for convention and conference hosting too. Orlando International Airport is a bustling hub, connecting visitors to the rest of Florida and the world. The geography of Orlando is flat, and the terrain outside the city is flat and swampy. Its inland location means it is protected from hurricanes, and enjoys a sub-tropical climate with humid summers.

The Orlando residential market recovered fast, and inventory is low, so prices are on the rise, and the best opportunities are gone. However, Orlando is always a sound long term investment. In July 2013 the median home price hit $153,000 which is the first time it crossed the $150,000 mark since 2008. There are a few months of inventory on the market and typically most properties are going to closing within 90 days. At the top end of the Orlando market there are a wide range of mega mansions, varying in size, style and price, from $5 million right up to the top home at $15 million. There are some wonderful properties in the $700,000 to $3 million range, including lakeside estates around $870,000 which seem like good lifestyle value for money. But at the other end of the market $250,000 can get you a decent three bedroom family home, or for $180,000 you can buy a comfortable family condo in a resort with short term rental programs. The most affordable entry options include 'condotels' where you can snap up a studio for $99,000.

Orlando is always a popular investment destination for people all over the world. A future development of the area around the Orlando Airport, called Medical City, is going to be a big new draw for Orlando. It will be a major hub for domestic and international medical tourism and may offer good opportunities for investment. Many of the biggest presences in the medical industry in Florida will be there: UCF (University of Central Florida), VA (Veterans Administration) Hospital, Research Center, Children's Hospital, etc. And this will bring doctors, researchers, and surrounding support staff to the area.

Kissimmee

> Population: 59,000
> Condo: $90,000 - $340,000
> Family Home: $150,000 - $3.4M
> Waterfront: N/A
> Investment Potential Rating: ***
> Nearest International Airport: Orlando International
> Airport (15 mins by car)

Kissimmee is technically the closest community to Disneyworld, and its close proximity to the attractions at Lake Buena Vista (home of Disneyworld), and Orlando make it a popular tourism destination. The city is a family orientated one, with plenty of kid-friendly activities, themed restaurants and theatres, swamp tours and outdoor attractions. Kissimmee has a pleasant downtown centred around Kissimmee Lakefront Park. An interesting feature is the Monument of States, which is made of minerals from every state and many different nations. Look out for the murals depicting the town's past as a cattle capital, where present-day rodeos and cattle auctions keep the town rooted.

Home prices in Kissimmee rose 32 percent from 2012 to 2013, the highest rise in the Central Florida region[18], indicating that the market is rising rapidly, and limited inventory—only three months worth—will continue to push them higher. Recently the New York Times ranked Kissimmee the third best place to buy a vacation home in the country based on price and location. In the Kissimmee market there are a handful of properties above $2 million, but most of the luxury market lies between $1 million and $1.8 million, which can buy a stunning single family home. At the other end of the market though, you can buy a home at $160,000 which might be a good long-term investment. In order to rent to holiday makers you would certainly need to spend closer to $200,000. $250,000 will get you a well appointed four bedroom family home. In the Condo market, the luxury end has few properties, with $340,000 being the top of the market for a three bedroom luxury condo. $200,000 will get you a spacious family condo, and it's possible to buy a small two bedroom condo in a resort with a pool for around $100,000.

FINDING A REAL ESTATE PROFESSIONAL

The professional you choose to assist you in your Florida property search is, hands down, the single most important decision you'll make other than your choice of eventual home. The right Realtor will have a comprehensive understanding of the local market, a lot of experience in dealing with the intricate details of international property transactions, and a keen sense of how to guide you through the whole process while staying focused on your unique requirements.

Buying a property is a several stage process, involving many people who should be making their best effort on your behalf. In the end, the process starts and ends with the Realtor you choose, as their role in representing you and your interests is the most critical in our opinion. It is imperative that you trust them to put forward their best effort, and provide you with excellent advice and expertise on one of the biggest decisions you have to make. Because of the possibility of litigation, some Realtors shirk what we believe is their professional responsibility to make suggestions, recommendations, and be pro-active in solution-finding. For example, they might give a list of professionals for the client to choose from: lenders, closing agents, inspectors, contractors, etc. And not share anything about the quality of their work and track record. We believe this is cumbersome, even for the savvy domestic buyer. We believe a Realtor should go the extra mile in putting in the groundwork and offering their personal opinion and experience on whom they believe to be the absolute best person for the job. We strive to be as informative and as transparent as possible. When obstacles do arise the best team will ensure that everyone can put their heads together and find new, and perhaps better, solutions.

Although we state this earlier it warrants repeating that hiring a real estate professional to work on your behalf and negotiate for your interests does not cost you anything. Realtors are paid at the time you make your purchase out of the proceeds of the seller.

What's the Difference Between a Realtor, a Real Estate Agent, and a Broker?

Throughout this book you see we emphasize again and again that you must choose the best **Realtor** you can find. This is an important question to understand and it's critical to know how to differentiate when you begin your search for a professional to represent you. Here are the definitions of each of these types of professional:

Real Estate Agent

This is a licensed real estate professional who has passed their real estate exam. Their job description is to assist and advise buyers and sellers in marketing and purchasing property. **If they are solely a licensee and not a Realtor,**

this person has no access to the MLS, and thus has no more access to information than you do through internet sources. Since the MLS is the most definitive and comprehensive source of real estate data, this is a big shortcoming in our opinion.

Real estate agents (as well as Realtors) can't actually accept remuneration in a property deal, i.e. handle the cash, unless they are a **licensed broker**. They facilitate deals on behalf of a broker. Therefore, agents can only sell property if they work for a real estate broker, or brokerage. Agents cannot list properties for sale, only assist and advise in the buying and marketing of them. An agent's job includes helping to arrange inspections, structuring contracts, and negotiating for your interests, so the agent needs to be experienced and knowledgeable in all these areas.

Realtor

This term is trademarked by the National Association of Realtors (NAR). This means that only real estate agents registered with NAR are allowed to call themselves Realtors. **And only Realtors have access to the MLS, have signed up to the association's code of ethics, and participate in regular training and continuing education.** The majority of real estate agents in Florida are signed up to the National Association of Realtors, if you find an agent you like who isn't signed up, we would ask them why not. Those who are designated Realtors, will have access to a wealth of information, support networks, and listings that those who choose not to sign up will not have access to.

To become a member of the NAR, you need to join your local real estate board or association. New NAR members must take an online course on the ethics code and pass an exam. Current members are required to take an online ethics refresher course every four years and adhere to standards of practice. The official ethics code is revised yearly to reflect the latest issues in real estate law and practice, and its core message is to "treat all parties honestly".

Real Estate Broker

A broker is a licensed professional who is qualified to handle all the elements already discussed above, as well as the financial part of real estate transactions. The broker is a real estate agent (in other words assists in selling and marketing) that has had more formal education. Agents must work under a broker's umbrella, and that broker takes legal responsibility for any action by the agent. Any mistakes or illegality on the agent's part is the legal responsibility of the broker. Brokers usually earn significantly more money than agents, and very often are their own bosses, with agents working under them, but also have much more legal liability and responsibility. **Again it is important to articulate here that while all brokers must have their real estate license, they may not necessarily be a Realtor.** If you choose to work with a broker be sure they are also Realtor.

WHAT IS A BUYER'S AGENT?

A buyer's agent is a Realtor you select to represent you when you want to buy a property. There are some key points we want to make about this relationship.

SELLING A PROPERTY? YOU NEED AN EXCLUSIVE AGENT/BROKER

Here in Florida when a client is selling a property, there is an exclusive contract called a listing agreement where you elect to work with one agent/broker on the sale of your house for a defined amount of time.

BUYING A PROPERTY? IT'S YOUR CHOICE: WORKING WITH MANY REALTORS VS. CHOOSING AN EXCLUSIVE BUYER'S AGENT

When it comes to the buy side, however, it is not uncommon in Florida for people to elect to view properties with one or more Realtors. It is not a general practice to sign a buyer's agreement to work with only one buyer's agent. We have countless stories about how often this leads to misunderstandings and confusion amongst the parties involved, but even more germane is the fact that **if**

you establish an excellent working relationship with a qualified Realtor, we feel it really works in your favour to work with them exclusively throughout the process. *(Remember: In Florida all Realtors have access to MLS so they are using the same database, containing all available listings.)*

Why an Exclusive Buyer's Agent Works Best

A very good Realtor is investing a lot of time on your behalf, especially when you are a foreign buyer, and they only get compensated at the time of a sale. We feel it is just plain good business practice to be fair, open, honest, and respectful of everyones' time. In this context that translates to working with just one Realtor, and if you meet others along the way making it clear up front that you are already represented. Anyone who is a true professional will really appreciate this clarity. Besides, if you are viewing properties in the same geographic area with various Realtors, you are likely creating more work and undue stress for yourself. In that situation no one person has the benefit of getting the full context of what you like and don't like. Therefore, in a way you are handicapping the multiple realtors you work with, preventing them from being able to effectively advise you on the big picture of this decision.

A BUYER'S AGENT IS "YOUR" AGENT

There is another key factor to weigh in at this point, and that is that **in the state of Florida, unless it is specifically specified in a buyer's agreement, an agent is working for the transaction, not for you specifically as the buyer.** The agent is known as a transaction agent. Within our brokerage, we feel it's preferable to work with Buyer's Agreements so that our clients can be sure that we have a fiduciary responsibility to them. This scenario is known as working under single agency, and is the more transparent and preferable way to do business. We believe it is much healthier for you to choose one person that you know will do a great job for you, and then sign a Buyer's Agreement with them so that you are guaranteed that the Realtor be a single agent, i.e. an agent representing one party in a transaction. The contract should lay out the geographic area your agent will represent you in, his/her responsibilities throughout the property search, as well as how long he will represent you for.

Please see the appendix for an example of a Buyer's Agent Agreement.

MORE ON TRANSACTION AGENTS VS. SINGLE AGENTS

To further articulate the distinction between working with a transaction agent vs. a single agent we want to provide a picture of the fiduciary duties a Realtor would have with you in either scenario:

The *transaction* agent does not advocate the interests of either the buyer or the seller. The standards of conduct expected of them are to deal with you with honesty, fairness, reasonable care and skill, and to disclose what is required. They must present offers/counter offers in a timely manner, assist parties in the closing of the transaction, keep parties fully informed, advise parties to obtain expert advice or counsel on matters outside their realm, and disclose all material facts affecting a property's value. They are expected to protect the confidences of both parties in matters that would materially disadvantage one party over the other. They consider you to be a customer, not a client.

A *single buyer's* agent is hired to do a job under a written Buyer's Agreement. With this contract you become more than a customer, you become a client. This formalizes the working relationship and increases their fiduciary responsibilities to you. In addition to the responsibilities outlined under the role of a transaction agent, a single buyer's agent must carry forward with:

Skill, Care, and Diligence

Your Realtor is expected to do his/her job with diligence and reasonable competence. Competence is generally defined as a level of real estate marketing skills and knowledge comparable to those of other practitioners in the area.

Loyalty

The duty of loyalty requires the agent to place the interests of the client above those of all others, particularly the agent's own. This standard is particularly relevant whenever an agent discusses transaction terms with a prospect.

Obedience

An agent must comply with the client's directions and instructions, provided they are legal. An agent who cannot obey a legal directive, for whatever reason, must withdraw from the relationship. If the directive is illegal, the agent must also immediately withdraw.

Confidentiality

An agent must hold in confidence any personal or business information received from the client (you) during the term of employment. An agent may not disclose any information that would harm your interests or bargaining position, or anything else you wish to keep secret.

Full Disclosure

An agent has the duty to inform the client of all material facts, reports, and rumors that might affect the client's interests in the property transaction.

CRITICAL MATERIAL FACTS FOR DISCLOSURE INCLUDE:

- The agent's opinion of the property's condition

- Information about the other parties' motivations and financial situation

- Adverse material facts including: property condition, title defects, environmental hazards, and property defects.

What Realtors Bring to the Table

Although all Realtors (though not all real estate agents as discussed previously) have access to MLS listings, experienced Realtors know how to skillfully search the database to find the best homes within the buyer's price range. Realtors also know how to read the subtle language in listing descriptions. A "newer roof" was probably replaced 10 years ago. A "charming" home might be a code word for a fixer-upper. A buyer's agent can narrow the listings down to a dozen good fits for the client. Then the Realtor can call the sellers' agents to arrange for showings. When it's time to look at the homes, the buyer's agent provides a crucial, objective opinion. Homebuyers have the habit of falling in love with a property because it has a great view or a huge kitchen, and may overlook other important considerations how the location plays into the lifestyle goals, or less favourable characteristics like lousy plumbing or a leaky roof. The buyer's agent can help the homebuyer see the whole picture such as repair costs, the neighbourhood, the local school system, taxes and so on, and they're not blinded by one or two superficial features.

Working with a buyer to select a handful of properties to look at is possibly the easiest part of the job of the Realtor. Once the buyer has found a home that he or she likes, the buyer's agent become your counsel on many fronts. First, they are the point of contact for all price negotiations. The buyer's agent knows how much other homes are selling for in the neighbourhood and will negotiate for the fairest price.

Once the buyer and seller enter into a Contract for Sale and Purchase, the Realtor will arrange for a professional home inspection so the buyer can learn about the house beyond what is superficially visible while walking through. These are typically very thorough and include things like the foundation, plumbing, roof, heating, cooling and electrical systems as well as appliances. He or she may also schedule termite and/or mould inspections. Sometimes it is prudent to have a separate inspector for the pool/spa system and air conditioning, when they are significant components. Based upon the contract used, when the inspection reports come back, either the seller will be responsible for making repairs, or the Realtor will help the homebuyer renegotiate or withdraw the offer. Then the Realtor will walk the homebuyer through the closing process, preparing all of the documents to complete the transaction.

LOCAL KNOWLEDGE IS KEY TO SERVING YOUR BEST INTERESTS

As always, local knowledge is what it's all about. Even in our own home market of Sarasota, the variations in lifestyle offered, price, and rental potential vary neighbourhood to neighbourhood, and even street to street in some cases. Only a local, well informed, and experienced Realtor can know the intricacies and nuances of any particular market, and how that will affect the outcome and lifestyle for the buyer. And a local agent with years of experience is likely to trade on the back of their reputation, and therefore operate reputably towards everybody involved in the deal, in order to ensure repeat business from all concerned.

Local Realtors also have the added benefits of historical market knowledge and insider details about properties. They may know some of the more subtle information which only comes from being a local, such as:

● If a property is poorly built, or is much older than it appears or is being listed as

● Has had problems in the past

- Was purchased at too high a price

- When the home was last on the market

- They may have been inside properties you are comparing in the past

- They may have knowledge of local homes about to come on the market

- They may know areas that have issues such as poor drainage, high water levels, poor soil, ground pollution, or unsavoury neighbours

- They may have an intimate knowledge of the town's zoning laws and restrictions or planning that has been passed and will affect the home you're looking at

- They may have knowledge of the particular departments of the city administration, how easy or hard it is to get planning and change restrictions

- They may know if a developer is in trouble financially.

In our own experience it is imperative to find an agent who is a skilled negotiator. There are thousands of agents out there but those who have the people skills, understanding and communicative ability to finesse the finer details of a deal with consummate professionalism, smoothing the obstacles and potential problems before they arise, are few and far between. Many times it's the smallest of details that can derail a real estate deal. We also always advise you to search for an agent who is full time, one that has dedicated him or herself to the profession, and is not doing it as an avocation or hobby. Part time agents are ten-a-penny, but if you've got a deal in the making you want the agent to have their full attention on making sure it goes through. As with all deals, time is of the essence for real estate transactions.

Investments in Florida Realtor Referral Program

In the following section of this book we provide you with a very thorough set of guidelines to empower you to research, interview, and engage a Realtor who will do the best job for you, however we also have many clients who request our professional experience to select one for them. **As an added resource to our readers, we offer our Investments in Florida Realtor Referral Program as one of the best ways to find a Florida Realtor. These individuals have all been personally pre-assessed by us, show the skill and experience we demand in an agent, and are experts in their region. Please go to** *www.InvestmentsInFlorida.com* **to have us hand select a professional who meets your criteria.**

Checklist for Choosing a Realtor

By virtue of knowing the market, the geography, and the inventory intimately, a seasoned Realtor will effectively listen to your criteria and quickly come up with the best matches for you. This skill is honed by years of experience, providing a much more efficient (and fun!) buying experience for buyers. A quality Realtor will keep this process as transparent as possible, and keep you informed, updated and connected.

Here are the types of topics you can research preliminarily by reading the Realtor's website, or checking through their profiles on places like Zillow or Trulia, so you can begin to understand their qualifications and find out who you would like to talk to further:

1. How long has the agent lived and worked in the area?

2. Is real estate the agent's full-time profession?

3. What types of awards, recognition or designations has the agent earned for their work?

4. Does the agent have good references/ recommendations? These are a really good indication of the agent's calibre

5. Does he or she have CIPS certification? (See our certification section for more details about why this is important)

6. Is he or she Transnational Referral Certified?
(See certification section)

7. Does he or she have significant experience in
international transactions?

8. Does he or she speak your own language? This is
obviously a massive help if your English isn't top notch

9. Does the agent have a good biography? It's surprising
to us how many agents don't have a biography on their
site. You want to know their depth of knowledge and
experience right up front, and if it's not there, we'd
want to know why. Good agents should have very
specific biographies meeting the very specific needs of
their clients

10. Is the agent's own website tailored to the international
market and buyer? There should at least be some
information about the agent's international experience

11. Is the agent well-traveled? Not critical, but in our
opinion the most travel-educated Realtors are also the
Realtors with the most understanding of other cultures,
and most ability to finesse cross-cultural deals

12. Does the agent have a team in place? You want
the agent to have a good network of experts and
professionals on hand, so you are accessing the
expertise of the entire team when you hire the agent

13. Does he or she own property him or herself?

Interviewing a Realtor

Once you've done your research, it's time to screen the Realtors you've short listed. We strongly suggest you have a personal phone call, video conference, or meeting with at least two or three people so that you get a feel for who would be the best match for you. In addition to the questions we outlined above, here are some key topics to discuss with them:

1. **Ask them to discuss their perspective on the current market.** This will help you to get a sense for how knowledgeable they are, and be a great education for you to have the most up-to-date sense of the market you are interested in

2. **Ask them to share what they do to ensure a smooth process for their foreign clients.** The Realtor should be able to describe going above and beyond to communicate, involve and motivate all the relevant parties to get the deal done as efficiently and effectively as possible. They should know that for many global buyers, English is not their first language and buying and selling real estate in their home country may differ extensively. While it may be hard to know specifically, there are clearly signals which will let you know if they will be a good communicator and steward in the transaction. For example, if the Realtor does not speak your native language, do they

speak slowly enough so that you can understand? Do they write out responses via email so that you can read, think about, and even use an online translator to understand?

3. **Ask them to tell you about the last three clients they had who were investors. What were they looking for and how did they help them?** The agent should be able to clearly differentiate between different types of investors, i.e. those looking purely for long-term appreciation, those looking for short-term cash-flow returns, and those seeking a lifestyle choice or combination of the above. The agent should have a detailed understanding of how these differ

4. **Ask for some references they might have from international clients they've helped invest in Florida real estate?** The agent should be able to prove his or her track record of helping foreign investors, and should have excellent relationships with former clients

5. **Ask if they have good relationships with lenders? Who are they?** Most good agents will have well established working relationships with specific individuals who work for lenders, and are familiar with working with global buyers. This will help to smooth the process of getting financing for you

6. **Ask them to share a bit about the team of professionals they have in place to make sure all facets of the purchase are handled with expertise?**
Your Realtor won't have all the answers. He or she will be a good generalist who then engages the professionals necessary to make the process smooth. He or she might not necessarily have all the in depth legal details of your unique situation, but he or she should know, and have a good working relationship with, someone who is the expert you need for that particular part of the transaction. The agent should be able to detail relationships with attorneys, immigration lawyers, tax specialists, inspectors, surveyors, pest inspectors, and property managers whom they have worked with many times and consider to be excellent

Real Estate Professional Certifications

The critical qualification you should look for in a Realtor is that they are a **Certified International Property Specialist** (CIPS). The CIPS designation is the most highly regarded certification for real estate professionals and only awarded to those who show global perspective in their business and a distinct understanding of global buyers.

In addition to this certification, we would always recommend that you choose a buyer's agent who is **Transnational Referral Certified**. The goal of this certification is to prepare real estate professionals to make and receive referrals using the Transnational Referral system developed by the International Consortium of Real Estate Associations (ICREA).

The National Association of Realtors defines the value of the designations it awards succinctly: "When you see initials like these behind a realtor's name, it means that this person is a committed professional, not content just to take the courses needed to get and maintain a real estate license, but determined to improve their professional skills and the quality of service they provide to their clients. They have devoted time to attending advanced educational courses and have taken examinations to earn these designations."

Below are the other main designations that you might come across. There are many more that you can read about on the National Association of Realtor's website. *www.realtor.org.*

Accredited Buyer Representative designation is awarded to real estate practitioners who complete a comprehensive two-day Real Estate Buyer's Agent Council course in buyer representation. Agents have to demonstrate practical experience by completing and closing five real estate transactions as a buyer's representative.

ARM

Accredited Residential Manager is the designation awarded to specialists who manage residential property, from rental apartment complexes, to mobile homes, condominiums, and single-family homes.

CBR

Certified Buyer Representative Realtors with this designation are taught to both help buyers find their desired property, and to negotiate for that property in a non-adversarial manner.

CIPS

CIPS – Certified International Property Specialist

Those with the CIPS designation are relied upon as a resource for experts in the international real estate market as they have completed an intensive seven day program focusing on critical aspects of transnational transactions, including: currency and exchange rate issues, cross-cultural relationships, regional market conditions, investment performance, tax issues and more.

RSPS

Resort and Second-Home Specialist.

This designation allows buyers and sellers to have confidence in the ability of a Realtor to assist them with their search for a resort or second-homes search.

SRES

Seniors Real Estate Specialist. Realtors with the "SRES" designation help seniors make wise decisions about selling the family home, buying rental property or managing the capital gains and tax implications of owning real estate. By earning the "SRES" designation, the Realtor has demonstrated that they have the requisite knowledge, experience and expertise to be a senior's real estate specialist and counselor.

(Information provided by *Realtor.org*)

The Final Decision: 3 Final Factors to Look For

1. Relationship

The primary thing to look for in your search for a Realtor is the right relationship. Relationships are about earning trust, and if the Realtor you choose can earn your trust from the beginning, it's an indicator that he or she will be able to do the same with other people. Your Realtor should also be able to relate to your situation and be able to demonstrate that they've worked with similar people, or people in similar situations. You can ask all the questions you want of any Realtor, but you want to have the synergy of working with someone who gets what you're about and what you're looking for.

2. Focus on Lifestyle

By buying Florida real estate you are investing in a lifestyle more than anything. Your Realtor should understand not only what that investment means to you, but the unique nuances of what you're looking for, and how you want to live in and use the property.

3. Thought Provoker

Your Realtor should be able to help you think through the process of buying real estate in Florida. They should be asking you plenty of questions, and they should want you to be actively thinking through what you really want and what kind of property will fit your lifestyle.

THE BUYING PROCESS

INTERNATIONAL SALES

In our experience there seems to be a good deal of misinformation out there about international sales. Buyers coming from other countries understandably have a fair amount of apprehension about what is involved, not knowing the process. But often Realtors also have concerns over the details of international sales. To be totally honest, **an international sale in the state of Florida pretty much follows the same process as a regular sale. There are a few more considerations surrounding movement of money, perhaps, but that's about all. If the buyer is a cash buyer then these minor complications are reduced. If the deal is to be financed there are a few more hoops to**

jump through. But overall the process is as simple and straightforward as any home purchase in America. It just requires an agent who is a good steward of the process, and has experience making sure all the due processes are observed speedily and efficiently.

The first step, after the recommended engagement of a buyer's agent (see section on buyers' agents) is usually to set out to find a property. Please see the previous sections on identifying the right area and property for you. This section will guide you through the process of the purchase.

Showings and Open Houses

We have met many of our clients—including some global buyers—when they visited an open house we were hosting. Open houses, we've been told, are not common in some European countries so it's probably a good idea to explain them here. In addition to giving you a good perspective on what is available in the market at what price point, they offer an opportunity for you, as a buyer, to meet and interview potential Realtors.

Some Realtors hold a listing open so that members of the public can come and view the house. Agents' opinions on the effectiveness of holding a house open to attract potential buyers are mixed. Some find that open houses can attract people not really interested in buying, only "lookers" who are curious to see the inside of the house. In our opinion there can't be any harm in getting some exposure for a listing. As a buyer, open houses offer a good opportunity to get a feel for the market, really understand what you can afford, and to compare properties in your price range.

Once you have found a Realtor that's going to do a great job for you, you should continue to look at open houses for your own education. **However as a professional courtesy and to be sure that your best interests will be served, you should let other Realtors who are hosting open houses know that you're working with a buyer's agent on a purchase.** You may be pleasantly surprised to learn they'll answer questions more candidly, and with greater detail once they know this, as they will take you more seriously as a buyer.

When you are interested in seeing specific properties your Realtor will make the showing appointments. Usually the owners of the house are out while you're shown the property. Sometimes the sellers' agent will be present to answer your questions about the property and give you more information. Your Realtor should also be fairly well informed and have done their homework on the property. If the seller's agent isn't present they should leave you a listing sheet with all the property's details. Make sure you make notes of all the things you like, all the things you don't, and all the things you need further information on.

Mortgage Pre-approval

The other key step in buying a home is of course having financing in place if you need it. Before you start your property hunt in earnest it's a really good idea to get pre-approved for a mortgage, just in case you see something you really like. Without pre-approval you'll most certainly not be the seller's first choice should there be several offers, and you won't really know for sure that you can even afford the property, or get a mortgage.

Please note: pre-qualified is not the same thing as pre-approved. Pre-qualified means you've given a lender your income details and financial commitments and they've estimated what you can afford. Pre-approved means they've actually checked your credit report, and your debt to income ratio, and properly analyzed your financial situation. Once they've done this you're given a pre-approval letter. This can certainly help in sealing the deal when in negotiations with a seller, and indicates that there's a really good chance you will get a mortgage and the sale will go through.

Making an Offer

Once you've found the right property, read through the Seller's Disclosure, and are ready to make a move on it, it's time to make an offer. In Florida this is done with a formal contract that lays out the specific requirements and terms on the part of the buyer and seller. Some Realtors may approach the seller's Realtor first with an oral offer, to see how the other party responds before they take the time to put anything in writing. From our perspective, we strongly encourage all offers to be presented in writing from the beginning. Offers that come in writing are generally more seriously considered by virtue of the fact that the terms are in writing.

AUTHOR'S NOTE

WHAT IS A SELLER'S DISCLOSURE?

In Florida it is the homeowner's responsibility to disclose any issues or material defects not readily visible or known to a Buyer. Your Realtor typically obtains the Seller's Disclosure form from the Seller's agent before constructing an offer. This information will help you to see if there are any details about the condition of the property that may affect the value you want to offer.

Contracts

IN FLORIDA, REALTORS PRIMARILY WORK WITH ONE OF TWO TYPES OF CONTRACTS:

- The Florida Realtors/Florida Bar Residential Contract for Sale and Purchase is the name of one of the documents used by Realtors to put together an offer. The standard contract provides that if there are issues uncovered during the inspection with warranted items—i.e. items which affect the integrity of the property such as a broken roof tile which could lead to a roof leak—the seller is obligated to make repairs of the warranted items (up to a limit agreed upon during the negotiation of the contract). The standard contract, if not otherwise specified, provides a default of 1.5 percent of the purchase price for repairs. Non-warranted items refer to cosmetic issues, such as a discoloration of floor coverings, wallpaper, or window treatments. See the appendix for an example of the most recent version of this contract for exact verbiage defining warranted and non-warranted items.

- The Florida Realtors/Florida Bar **"As-is"** Residential Contract for Sale and Purchase. Typically bank-owned, investor-owned, estate sales, or older homes will be marketed and sold "As-is". This means that should the inspection report reveal issues with the house, the seller is not obligated under the contract to make those repairs.

While the perception is that once the seller agrees to a buyer's purchase price they will have no further responsibility for the property, our experience dictates that this is not the reality. **In many situations, we actually prefer using the "as-is" contract with our buyers as we believe it protects them more fully should they decide they do not want to proceed with the purchase for any reason during the due diligence process.**

There are two primary reasons we prefer to work with an "as-is" contract. First, this is the only contract that allows the buyer to receive a full refund of deposit should they determine that the property is not right for them. Second, the seller will most likely agree to make repairs that any subsequent buyer is likely to find issue with as well. For example, if a house has a termite problem, the seller will likely take action to resolve it, as nearly any future buyer would not proceed with a purchase with the knowledge that an active infestation exists. Should anything major about the house be revealed during the due diligence period, it will not only be a concern for you, but for most every other buyer as well. So the onus is pushed back to the seller—although they are not obligated to do anything under the terms of the contract—to make the needed repairs or reduce the purchase price accordingly as the problem is not going to disappear and their goal is to sell.

The purchase contract should be drawn up by your Realtor with all the details and signed by you. In many cases, buyers are asked to put up "earnest money" which is a small amount of the deposit, to demonstrate that you are serious about the purchase. Do bear in mind, if your offer is accepted and you then later pull out of the deal without the necessary provisions in the contract, you'll forfeit that money.

HERE'S WHAT THE CONTRACT SHOULD INCLUDE:

- **The price you're offering for the property**

- **The percentage or value of the earnest money you will put down.** Just as a rule of thumb, many sellers like to see ten percent put down for the total deposit. This may take the form of the initial earnest money deposit up front (within three days usually), and the remainder of the deposit usually being due within ten days of signing, or sometimes at the end of the due diligence period

- **Response time to the offer by the seller.** The contract should set out in writing the date and time by which you expect a response to the offer. This ensures all parties have a clear idea of how long the offer is valid and helps to keep things moving along, or have a definitive end point

- **Proposed closing date**. In Florida the majority of closings occur within 30 to 45 days of going to contract. This can vary greatly, however, depending on specific circumstances

- **Number of days allotted for due diligence**. The default amount in the standard contracts is 15 days

- **Repair limits.** This is applicable if you're not using an "as-is" contract

- **Financing contingency and time frame**. These should be included to protect yourself if you don't get the mortgage deal you'd hoped for. It should be stated in the contract that the sale will only go through if your mortgage gets approved, and specify the maximum interest, and terms of the mortgage that are acceptable to you

- **Inventory of items included in the purchase**. Typically, major appliances stay with the property, unless otherwise specified, including: fridges, sinks, stoves, microwaves and often the washer and dryer. It is important to be sure this is clearly spelled out, though, as we have had the experience of very large transactions becoming contentious over these relatively small things.

Obviously the seller doesn't have to accept the offer, even if you offer the full price of the listing. And sellers are under no obligation to explain why they reject a particular offer. Usually we find most buyers hear back with in a day or so, and in most cases the seller will let you know if the offer was too low, which is where the negotiation begins! You can bide your time at this point and gamble on seeing what happens, or increase your offer hoping to secure the property immediately.

Offer Acceptance

The minute you learn your offer has been accepted ranks up there as one of life's most exciting moments. It is important to keep grounded, however, in the fact that there are still many steps in the due diligence stage that may uncover issues or problems on either side. As with much in life, when it comes to real estate deals, the devil is in the details.

After your offer is accepted, if you haven't already put down earnest money you will be expected to do so on the signing of the contract. Always be aware that earnest money could be at risk if the seller does what he or she is required to by contract and you do not. Depending on how the terms were set out in the contract, usually within the first few days after execution of the contract you'll put down the remaining deposit for the property. Then it's time to begin checking off the contingencies set out in your contract, which is where the skill of your Realtor, and the quality of the team he or she's assembled becomes paramount, beginning with the home inspection.

Home Inspection

An inspection checks the condition of the house itself. Even with a brand new house inspections are critical. With new homes there is usually a guarantee against anything that is wrong, so it may turn out to be really beneficial to get an inspection done. **If the "As-Is" contract is in place, the buyer's decision to move forward will usually be contingent on the inspection being satisfactory. If the inspection is not satisfactory, the buyer may want to pull out, or some negotiation may be required between buyer and seller to find a solution both are comfortable with.** Some things may need to be fixed, but really the main purpose is to provide an outline of the state of the house so the buyer understands what they're buying. There are so many issues that can hide in houses, and even if they're not deal-breakers you need to know what potential costs or issues you're taking on. We feel it is important to set the expectation that no house is perfect, even brand new homes, and it is quite normal for there to be in the range of $1000-$2000 worth of work needed. Again, if these are material defects then they will generally be covered by the seller if the standard purchase contract is being used (see explanation above).

Your Realtor should be able to provide you with choices for experienced, professional inspectors and have a preferred inspector they can personally recommend as an exemplary professional. It's important to make sure that the person who performs the inspection is truly independent and able to provide unbiased, objective information about the condition of the house. Your inspector should be certified by the American Society of Home Inspectors. (See our section on Professionals You Need.)

Here are the major areas the inspector will cover:

FOUNDATION

Checking if the foundation is sound. If there is a crawl space or basement they will check for signs of water damage, cracks that could indicate structural issues, and moisture.

CONSTRUCTION

The inspector will check if the property is well-constructed or not. While 90 percent of homes in the U.S. are made of wood, many homes in Florida are of concrete block construction. In a wooden home they will check if the wood is in good condition, with flashing to protect it. In a concrete block home they will check the quality of the construction, and that the blocks are not degrading. The condition of the roof, as well as windows and any other woodwork, exterior cladding and guttering, will also be checked.

PLUMBING

The inspection will check if the plumbing is fully functional, if there is evidence of leaks, and that all the pipe work is in good shape. For houses with wells and septic tanks, the inspection should include these as well.

HEATING AND COOLING SYSTEMS

The inspection will check the condition of the units, how soon they will need replacing, and check the temperature differential to see that the system is operating correctly. In some cases we may recommend that a specialist in heating and cooling do a separate inspection. For example, when there are multiple cooling systems in a home or there are signs that something is amiss.

ELECTRICAL

Check for any electrical problems or issues, flag any wiring that may need replacing. Identify any potential safety hazards.

INTERIOR

The inspection will check that floors are level, uncover any mildew concerns, and any drywall or finishing issues on the inside of the property, examine window and doors, and touch most things that move, open, close on the inside of the home.

The cost of an inspection in Florida usually ranges from $400 to $500. Please see the appendix for an example of an inspection report from a firm we regularly work with.

Pest Inspection

We always recommend that our clients have a pest inspection done when buying a property, for peace of mind. An average pest inspection costs $30-$50. In Florida these inspections check for Wood Destroying Organisms (commonly referred to as termites), rodent infestations, and also to scope out areas that can be sealed to prevent any rodents from gaining access to a home in the future. If termites are found they need to be treated by a pest expert. To those who are unfamiliar, this might seem like an overwhelming issue, but in fact the problem is not uncommon in Florida and there are well-defined solutions. Termite inspectors in Florida make a joke—there are two types of houses...those that have termites and those that will get termites. If the inspector finds any rodents inhabiting the property, they are typically removed through traps.

How Inspections Play into Insuring your Property

With any house you buy it's important to remember that the condition of the house will affect the insurance premiums too. In order to get the most accurate insurance quotes you must first have the completed inspection report. Insurance rates tend to be higher in Florida than in other places in the world. As soon as the inspection report is ready it is important to share it with the insurance agent because insurance premiums (the annual amount charged to insure the property) in Florida are set based on a combination of factors. The subset of the inspection reports that will be helpful to your insurance agent will be a four-point inspection (specifically roof, electric, plumbing and cooling/heating systems) and the wind mitigation inspection. Other aspects of the home that will likely play a role in the insurance rates will be the home's current condition, age, and cost to rebuild with the current finish, quality of materials, ceiling heights, etc. Proximity of the house to the water and a fire station may also play a factor.

If you are using the standard purchase contract, we would recommend an insurance addendum, so that if you get insurance quotes that may be beyond your budget or willingness to pay, you have another protection as the buyer to legally get out of the contract and get a return of your deposit. Another reason we like working with the "As-Is" contract is that no addition addendums are required. As long as you give notice during the due diligence period you can exit the contract for any reason and get a full return of deposit.

INSURANCE

Homeowners' Insurance

Homeowners' insurance helps pay to repair or rebuild your home and replace personal property due to a covered loss. A typical policy would include loss from theft and structural damage from fire, leaks, water discharge, fallen trees, or as a result of a storm. In our experience, the majority of claims tend to be for water leaks; from air conditioning systems, water heaters, plumbing and roofs, rather than the more dramatic possibilities. Mortgage lenders usually require homeowners' insurance as part of the mortgage terms. If you are getting financing you must at a minimum have a basic policy. Most policies include coverage for the house itself, as well as for the property inside the house.

The following are the key components of the standard homeowners' insurance policy:

- Dwelling

- Other Structures (shed, detached garage)

- Personal Property

- Loss of Use/Additional Living Expenses (if your house is uninhabitable after a covered loss)

- Personal Liability (if someone claims you caused them injury or property damage)

- Medical Payments (to others).

When you own a condominium, the structure will usually be insured by the condominium association and you will pay a portion of that cost through your association fees. You may then only need a policy that insures the interior portion—also known as "improvements and betterments"—of your unit and the contents of your condo.

Typically insurance policies include a "deductible" or excess, which is the amount of money that the homeowner contributes to the repair or replacement cost of property. Generally, the higher the deductible/excess the lower the annual premium. Be sure you thoroughly review the type of policy you purchase and ask any questions. It is important to have the proper insurance and understanding of what you purchased. In addition to the standard coverage you may want to discuss the relevance of additional coverage. Some examples include: identity fraud, pet liability, pool cages and screen enclosures, mould, sewer backup or valuable items such as jewelry.

Wind Policy

Wind or windstorm insurance generally is included as part of your Homeowner's Insurance, but we want to discuss the topic a bit more thoroughly here as we consider it an important aspect of your policy to understand. In much of Florida, we are susceptible to tropical storm or hurricane force winds. As such, we guide our clients to ensure they are fully informed about the wind coverage that is included in their insurance package. This includes providing them with information on how to help protect their home from damage, potentially reducing the costs of this portion of the insurance in the first place. Protecting your home may even reduce the payout towards your deductible/excess.

After Hurricane Andrew hit south Florida in 1992, municipalities around the state of Florida created higher standards to better protect homes from damage from winds and wind-borne debris. We refer to these as building codes. They include improved methods for attaching the roof to the house, reinforcing garage doors, installing windows that can withstand debris hurled at greater speeds, etc. The benefit of living in a home built to newer codes (or retrofitted with these features) is both a safer home and lower costs of insurance.

Older homes are more susceptible to wind damage as they are not made to resist as much wind as the newer builds. Examples of the types of damage that can occur from excess wind are having the shingles or roof ripped off, windows smashed from flying debris, garage doors or walls knocked down. Many older homes have incredible charm, character and features that newer homes may not have, so we are not discouraging you from looking at older homes, we just want you to know that there are measures you can take to help protect your home and reduce insurance costs. Some examples would be to install new windows that have impact glass or hurricane shutters. You can have hurricane straps added to your roof system, and also install a new impact-resistant garage door.

Building codes and building materials are both continually evolving. Have your Realtor, insurance professional, and home inspector help you understand the different trade-offs and costs associated with the different options. To provide an example to explain this point: You want to install a set of storm shutters (protection for windows and doors) and the cost is estimated at $6000, and you learn it will reduce your premium by $3000 per year. Most would consider this a good investment because the payback is 2 years. However if the same shutters cost $150,000 then the payback would be 50 years and probably not a good investment.

The World Meteorological Association will name any storm that has sustained winds over 39 mph. With wind insurance a standard deductible/excess is two percent for a named storm. (Note: for any other storm the deductible you have pre-chosen in your contract will apply). It is commonplace for the wind policy to use a percentage of the total coverage limit rather than a flat cost. For example, a wind policy for $250,000 with a two percent deductible/ excess means the insured pays the first $5,000 of repairs. Again, you can choose the amount of deductible/excess based on where you are and how much you are willing to pay in premiums. *Author's note: sometimes the mortgage company may limit the amount of deductible/excess you are allowed to have on the policy.*

Flood Insurance

A flood insurance policy protects your home against potential flood damage. The question of whether a property is in a flood zone comes up *all the time* from buyers. Even within our own real estate profession, however, many do not know how to respond accurately. In the past few years there have been numerous legislative and rate changes for homeowners' flood policies due to the National Flood Insurance Program (NFIP). Even information from the current seller of a property—especially if they have an older home—may not be applicable as they may themselves not be aware of how their property has been affected by the changes.

The bottom line? It is best to consult a trusted insurance professional at the very start of the due diligence process with any property you put under contract, to get an accurate flood insurance quote and explanation of flood zones.

When and Where it Can Flood

Let's dive into some basic explanations to help you get oriented to this topic in very simple terms.

Anywhere it rains, it can flood. There are two main types of flooding. The first scenario occurs when there is a tropical storm or hurricane that produces a tidal surge: such as when water from the Atlantic Ocean or Gulf of Mexico moves over the beach and onto normally dry land. The second happens with heavy, rapid rainfall when storm waters have nowhere else to go. In other words, the water drainage systems, lakes, rivers, and streams cannot absorb excess water fast enough and so it overflows onto land, streets, car parks, or neighborhoods and then into homes. Other conditions such as an outdated or clogged drainage system, or new development (a building, car park, or road) may also change the ability of the land to absorb excess precipitation and can result in a flood.

WHAT ARE FLOOD ZONES?

Every area in the United States is classified as a flood zone. What does that mean? Everyone lives in a flood zone—it's just a question of the degree of severity of the risk. You may live in a low, moderate, or high-risk area. While most perceive that the closer you are to bodies of water the greater the risk, there are more factors that come into play. You can be in an area of the mountains and experience flooding because water flowing from higher levels pools faster than it can drain or be absorbed.

While there are many codes used to define flood zones, there are two main categories: Special Flood Hazard Areas and Preferred Flood Zones.

WHAT IS A SPECIAL FLOOD HAZARD AREA?

Areas which are at a high risk for flooding are called Special Flood Hazard Areas (SFHAs). Most, if not all barrier islands around Florida are considered SFHAs, as are areas close to the coast and other bodies of water.

If you are in a SFHA and you are financing your property, flood insurance is required. If you pay cash it is optional, but again highly recommended. We personally advise everyone to get flood insurance.

If you are in a Special Hazard flood zone, an Elevation Certificate will be required to determine how high above or below the Base Flood Elevation (BFE) you are. BFE is the height, relative to the mean sea level, that has a one percent chance or greater of flooding in a given year as determined by FEMA and adopted by your local jurisdiction. Rates will go up sharply for each foot you are below the BFE, and will go lower for each foot you are above the BFE.

Where we live in Sarasota, all new homes within Special Hazard flood zones are required to be built with the first living floor at or above the Base Flood Elevation. This applies even to waterfront property.

Insurance professionals refer to Flood Insurance Rate Maps (FIRMs) to be able to identify which type of flood zone a property falls within based on its address. These maps are constantly being updated due to changes in geography, construction and mitigation activities, and meteorological events. Therefore, even though you may find sites available to the general public online that give flood zone codes, for truly accurate information you must contact your insurance agent or mortgage broker. These are the two parties who by contract have access to the definitive mapping site.

Another complexity that may affect flood insurance rates is the value and location of appliances/equipment in and around the house that service the home. Insurance companies may want to know how elevated the appliances are inside or outside the home, how many storeys exist in the home, and where the main living areas are.

Florida homeowners are able to purchase flood insurance through various providers, but by virtue of the National Flood Insurance Program (NFIP), *the federal government has standardized the rates so your annual cost will be the same irrespective of what insurance company you choose.* Currently, the maximum coverage available through the NFIP is $250,000 for the structure and $100,000 for the contents. The current annual cost if you are in a Preferred Flood Zone and is $414, with a $1000 deductible/excess for each claim.

One of our German clients purchased a home in 2013 on a barrier island about 200 metres from the Gulf of Mexico. Even though his home is in a Special Hazard Zone, he currently pays about $404 per year. The home was built in 2006 and the first living level (air conditioned space) is roughly eight feet above the base flood elevation.

Flood insurance normally requires a 30 day waiting period from the time you sign up before the coverage is effective. Exceptions are only made for certain circumstances such as if you're purchasing a home and there is a loan being taken out to finance the purchase.

You can find more details at: ***www.floodsmart.gov***.

Survey

The survey details the property dimensions and the location of the house and fixed structures on the site relative to the property lines. It shows the measurements of the walls of the structures, location of the driveway, decks, sheds, pools, AC units, and/or any existing fences. It will state the property address and the legal description as recorded with the municipality.

The closing agent reviews the details of the survey to determine if they adhere to setback requirements established by the municipality and/or neighborhood deed restrictions. Most closing agents will not bring up the survey with you unless they uncover a discrepancy. To give you an example from our real life experience: when the existing fence is installed in the neighbours garden, or a wall of the house is closer to the property line than is required by the setbacks in the neighborhood deed restriction, these are situations where the survey may be brought up. Some things have a simple solution that your closing agent can help you to resolve. Others are more complicated, and with many Florida contracts the seller is held accountable to "cure" any issues of title and survey, i.e. they have to find a solution.

Any lender will require a survey as they want to know as much as possible about the asset that secures the loan. It is not necessary to spend the money on a new one if a good one already exists. If the seller is able to provide a survey, your closing agent can advise you if it is of sufficient quality to use, so that you do not have to order a new one. We recently facilitated a transaction where the seller had the original, certified survey. However, because it was from 1986, the closing agent felt it was a prudent investment ($350-$450) to have a new survey done. If there is one that is usable, the closing agent will get an affidavit signed by the seller stating that there have been no changes to the property that would affect the distances between fixed structures and lot (site) line. (Meaning no changes to the footprint of the house, no fences added, and no new buildings have been added to the property.)

If you are paying cash, a survey is not required to close, but again we highly recommend it for our clients. You just never know when something concerning the boundaries or construction on your property is in violation of a restriction. **When you're making any real estate purchase we are proponents of ensuring that you as the buyer are fully informed on all fronts.** The survey is usually completed within five days of closing rather than as part of the initial due diligence, so if there are any issues that come up with the survey they tend to be late in the process. This has the potential to delay your closing date slightly, as by contract the seller typically has up to 30 days to convey marketable title (i.e. a title which is readily transferable since it is free from valid claims by outside parties).

We recently had a closing on a property where the title search revealed a tree permit from years earlier was still open with the municipality. This means a permit had been applied for to do something on the property years earlier, and it still had to be closed, i.e. signed off as being correct by the town. It created a problem—which was resolvable—but is a good example of things which can come up and hold up your sale. The skill and experience of your Realtor in this situation will help to keep things progressing and getting the checklist of to-do's done. If all comes up clean on the title search, then you are ready to close.

Appraisal

If you are financing your purchase an appraisal will be required by your lender to check the current value of the property. The market value differs from the recorded (assessed) value set by the municipality, so it's necessary for the lender to protect the money they are lending you by getting an independent assessment of what the property is worth at market value. Lenders have no control over the choice of appraisers; it is done at arm's length by a third party. The lender will require the appraised value to come out within a certain percentage of the amount being financed.

When paying cash it's not mandatory to have an appraisal, but is still highly recommended so you really know the true value of the property you're buying. We advise our buyers to make the appraisal part of the terms written into the due diligence part of the contract. When you are paying cash you may choose the appraiser. Appraisals usually cost between $300 and $500 dollars. Please see our section on Professionals You Will Need for more information on how to select a qualified appraiser.

AUTHOR'S NOTE

Appraisals are highly subjective. While we think the appraisal provides a good data point, we have many stories of how they throw off a whole deal because they come out unexpectedly low or high. While there are many competent appraisers, there are also those that really do not have the qualifications and experience in a given market to properly assess the property. When this happens it is a huge injustice for all parties who are part of the transaction.

In these situations where the appraisal is a "shocker" we guide our clients to all the information they have at their disposal to determine how much value they want to place on one appraisal. In today's environment both buyers and sellers have tremendous data available to them in terms of comparables provided by their Realtor through the MLS, and using sites like Trulia and Zillow. In the end, we feel that the best estimate of value is the price the seller and buyer agree to.

Title Insurance

When you buy a property, what you're really buying is the title. The title is evidence that the owner is in lawful possession of that property. One of the key ways Florida homeowners are protected is through title insurance. **This is a one-time fee paid at closing**, as opposed to other types of insurances that have yearly premiums.

Title Insurance, in essence, protects owners (and lenders when they are involved) from any possible claims that could come up from the property's past. These might include things such as another person claiming an ownership interest, improperly recorded documents, liens such as unpaid taxes, outstanding loans, and easements (where a third party is granted access to cross the property).

HOW DOES TITLE INSURANCE DIFFER FROM OTHER INSURANCE WE HAVE DISCUSSED?

Homeowners and Flood Insurance protects against potential future events and is paid for with monthly or annual premiums. A title insurance policy insures against events that occurred in the past of the real estate property and the people who owned it, for a one-time premium paid at the close of the escrow.

The title company performs a search to determine the title is clear and that there are no other claims to ownership. The findings of the search are summarized into a document called 'Commitment for Title Insurance'. This shows that the title company will be prepared to issue an insurance policy on the title once you own it.

Title insurance is required by lenders. If you are paying cash it is not actually mandatory, however our advice is that you get it. It just makes sense to have the guaranteed assurance that you are the owner. **In contrast with owning property in a lot of other countries, title insurance creates a clear ownership policy. A title insurance company is guaranteeing there are no other claims on your title, and they're so sure of that being the case, they are prepared to pay out serious sums of money in the event that they're wrong.**

The government sets title insurance rates, so they're not arbitrary. When you come to closing, the closing agent you use is paid primarily out of the title insurance fee.

There are generally two types of title insurance policies:

Owner's Title Insurance

This policy protects the homebuyer's interest. It is normally issued for the amount of the property's purchase price. Coverage means the insurance agency will pay out on all claims, which are proved valid, on the insured title.

Lender's Title Insurance

The mortgage lender usually requires the homebuyer to buy a lender's title insurance policy. This protects the lender's interest in the property. Lender's title insurance is issued for the loan amount of the mortgage.

HOW MUCH DOES TITLE INSURANCE COST?

The cost of title insurance is determined by the purchase price of the property. Under $100,000 the cost is $5.75 per thousand, above $100,000 the cost is $5.00 per thousand. So for example on a $500,000 dollar home, the cost of title insurance would be $2,500. This is a one-time premium, paid at closing, and never again until the next sale of the property. Costs for title insurance are standardized, the cost on a $500,000 home in Dade County (Miami) is the same as in Orange County (Orlando).

In Florida, if a property was previously sold within three years, the current buyer will receive a partial credit on the re-issue of a title policy for that same property. For example, one of our recent global buyers received a $2370 credit on the reissue of a title policy for his beachfront home because it had changed hands two years prior.

WHO COVERS THE COST FOR TITLE INSURANCE?

In Florida the party that covers the cost for title insurance varies depending on the county. Often it can be a point in the contract that is open for negotiation. The seller generally pays for the title insurance and chooses the closing agent (a title company or attorney) in the majority of Florida counties. The buyer usually pays for title insurance and chooses the closing agent in the following counties: Collier, Sarasota, Miami Dade, and Broward. In instances of bank owned properties, the seller always chooses and pays for the title insurance. This is usually true of new builds and new developments too.

AUTHOR'S NOTE

THE VALUE OF BEING ABLE TO CHOOSE THE CLOSING AGENT.

We recommend to our clients that if at all possible negotiate to have their choice of the closing agent. We personally believe a real estate attorney will be more thorough than a title company as it relates to turning over every stone on your behalf to be sure the transaction runs smoothly and you are protected. A title company tends to be more neutral. Please see the section on Closing Agents for more information.

WAYS TO HOLD TITLE

There are several options for how to hold title on your Florida real estate, however if you are financing you only have one option. Lenders require title to be in the individual's name(s). If you pay cash, some of the more common ways you can elect to hold title are as an individual, as a U.S. or foreign corporation, as a limited liability corporation (LLC), or as a trust. We will elaborate on some of these below, however, we want to begin by emphasizing two key points.

One, the biggest consideration for how to set up title is how each scenario will affect your tax liability, especially capital gains and estate tax. Estate tax (tax on your right to transfer property at your death) can be particularly onerous if not planned for up front. Second, the tax codes are generic, so it is really important to find out how your specific situation may be affected based on the tax treaties that exist between the U.S. and your home country. Many countries have tax treaties with the U.S., which can reduce or eliminate certain tax obligations in/to the U.S.

Each form of ownership has its tradeoffs—some large, some small. Our advice, as always, is to make an informed choice. Everyone's financial and personal circumstances are so unique; it's worth investing the few hundred dollars to find out whether the pros of using an LLC or foreign corporation to hold ownership make sense for you.

Below we illustrate some of the tax advantages and disadvantages of the most commonly used ways to own U.S. real estate available to nonresidents.

Individual Ownership

Taking title in the individual's name is the most frequently used option. It is the method that results in the least amount of U.S. income tax when a property is sold. If the property is held for at least one year before it is sold, the maximum tax is calculated at 15-20 percent (depending on the individual's tax bracket) of the profit. If the net income from any one year is greater than $250,000 there is an additional 3.8 percent tax on the gain.

However, this could be the most disadvantageous way of holding title if the non-resident dies while still owning the property. The estate tax is assessed on the fair market value of the property at the date of death of the owner. It is payable to the IRS no later than nine months after the date of death and, if not paid in a timely manner, it is subject to penalties and interest, which are payable in addition to the estate tax. For non-U.S. residents, the estate tax applies to property valued in excess of $60,000. The marginal rate for the estate tax imposed on the estate of decedents dying after December 31, 2012 is 40 percent.

U.S. Corporate Ownership

Non-residents are eligible to take title to U.S. real estate in the name of a U.S. corporation. Unlike individual ownership, the corporation does not get the preferential capital gains tax rate of 15 percent or 20 percent (depending on one's tax bracket) on long-term capital gains. If the property is located in Florida, then there is a state corporate income tax of 5.5 percent of profit in excess of $5,000 that must also be paid. The overall highest federal income tax rate for property in Florida held through a U.S. corporation is approximately 38 percent. Compared to the maximum individual tax rate of 15 percent-20 percent on the sale of property, the corporate income tax rate is very high. This is obviously a disadvantage of U.S. corporate ownership of real estate.

The potential advantage of U.S. corporate ownership of U.S. real estate is from the standpoint of U.S. estate taxes. Although the value of shares in a U.S. corporation owned by a nonresident is generally subject to U.S. estate tax upon the death of the owner, estate tax treaties with certain countries (for example, United Kingdom and Germany) provide for an exemption of these shares from the U.S. estate tax. This can be a substantial benefit for those nonresidents who qualify.

Foreign Corporate Ownership

This is a fairly rare choice of method to hold title, and brings with it some complications. But is worth knowing about as it may suit your unique personal situation, especially if you are older, don't have an income as such, and seeking to avoid estate tax. The foreign (non U.S.) corporation is subject to the same income tax rates as the U.S. corporation. The benefit of the foreign corporation lies with the U.S. estate tax. Unlike the U.S. corporation, all nonresidents are exempt from U.S. estate tax upon their death if the property title is held by a foreign corporation. The country of residence of the owner is irrelevant.

U.S. Limited Liability Corporation Ownership

U.S. limited liability companies have become increasingly popular as an alternative for ownership of U.S. real estate by nonresidents, due to their extreme flexibility. The limited liability company is a legal entity. The taxability of a limited liability company is dependent on several factors. A limited liability company with two or more members is taxed as a partnership, unless it has elected to be taxed in another manner, such as a corporation. If the limited liability company has only one member and it has not elected to be taxed as a corporation, then it is treated, for income tax purposes, as a "disregarded entity" and the owner is taxed directly. For example, if the owner of a single member limited liability company is a foreign individual, then the rules and tax rates applicable to foreign individuals will apply. The single member limited liability company will provide the owner with limited legal liability, but it will be taxed in the U.S. for income and estate tax purposes as if the company did not exist.

CLOSING PREPARATIONS

A day or two before closing, all parties involved in the transaction will receive a copy of the **Settlement Statement**. Also known as HUD Form 1, this form is a complete reconciliation of all the debits and credits (movement of money) among buyer, seller and vendors who are party to the transaction. It explains all of the settlement costs, and who pays whom, in detail. It will let you as the buyer know exactly how much money you need to bring to closing. Please see the appendix for an example of this document.

Estimating Purchasing Costs

To cover the purchasing costs (inspections, survey, title, appraisal, legal fees, title insurance premiums, taxes on transfer, recording fees), and mortgage taxes and fees (if applicable) you should estimate spending between one and three percent of the purchase price. All of these costs are one-time fees that are part of completing the transaction. When you are financing, your purchasing costs are a bit higher than when paying cash.

AUTHOR'S NOTE

What are taxes on transfer? Taxes on transfer, also referred to as document stamps, are a fixed rate for any property, at .07 cents per hundred dollars. So ,for example, on a $100,000 home it would come to $700. This is usually paid by the seller, but can be a negotiation point.

Things That Need to be in Place Prior to Closing Day

BALANCE DUE

In a cash closing, the buyer must bring to closing the difference between the amount he/she put down as a deposit and the purchase price, as well as any outstanding purchase or ownership costs that are due at closing. If the buyer is financing, this number is the purchase price and purchase costs, less the initial deposit(s) and amount of the mortgage. Typically the balance is paid via wire transfer, though some buyers still opt for a certified cheque.

PROOF OF INSURANCE (ONLY IF YOU ARE FINANCING)

A letter or statement showing you have taken out homeowners' insurance on the property. This is required by the lender. This is handled in advance of closing date as the policy has to be in place on the day of closing. Typically it is coordinated between the mortgage broker/lender, closing agent, and insurance broker.

UTILITIES

The buyer assumes the cost of utilities on the day of closing, thus he or she is responsible for establishing his or her own account for all utilities prior to that date. The Realtor can help with which companies to contact for services such as water/sewer, electric, cable (or satellite TV), telephone/ internet, and if applicable, gas. Also, if the buyer wants to continue using service providers that are in place for things such as pool cleaning and lawn care, these parties can be contacted as well to set up new account. For an in depth discussion of utilities and your choices in Florida please see our chapter on Owning a Home in Florida.

Closing Day

With increasing ease of travel and technology, closings are becoming less and less of an "event" done at a scheduled time and location with all parties in the same room. Many times sellers and buyers are signing documents on different days and at different locations, including anywhere around the world. Your closing can be conducted by email and mail if you can't be present. It's also worth noting that U.S. embassies provide notary services for foreigners.

If you are present at the closing you will possibly meet with the sellers (unless they have completed all the documents by mail), both Realtors, and often a real estate attorney (see later sections on professionals) to sign a huge mountain of paperwork. By the time you wade through and sign it all you'll be the proud owner of a title, a mortgage, and some shiny new house keys. **The day of closing is owned by the buyer. The buyer takes ownership and responsibility for taxes, insurance and utilities, and any other costs associated with home ownership.**

The closing itself will be run by a closing agent or real estate attorney. Whether you as the buyer, or the seller, choose the closing agent varies by county and can be negotiated in the contract. Please see our section on title insurance for more information on this. The fees for the closing agent's work are included in the title insurance costs. His or her job is to ensure that you understand each form you are signing.

Closing Forms

Here are some of the most important forms at closing for the buyer:

WARRANTY DEED

The piece of paper that officially transfers the title from the seller to the new owner. Florida is a title state, which means that you, rather than the lender, hold the title to the property.

LOAN PACKET (IF FINANCING)

There are numerous documents lenders require including the Mortgage Agreement, Truth in Lending Statement, and Promissory Note.

The time you spend at your closing is largely defined by whether you are paying cash or financing. In the cash scenario, you'll probably spend less than 30 minutes at your closing. If you are financing, the process is more time consuming as there are many financial and legal forms. You can spend around an hour working through all the required forms and signatures.

PROFESSIONALS YOU NEED & WHAT THEY DO

This section provides an orientation to the various professionals you may need to work with in a real estate transaction in Florida. **Since every successful real estate purchase experience starts and ends with choosing an excellent Realtor, please refer to the chapter earlier in the book for a comprehensive discussion of how to find the best Realtor for your needs.**

Over many years of working in real estate, we have interacted with hundreds of different real estate professionals, contractors and vendors. Over this time we have developed the philosophy that we will only work with people that we know, like and trust. The reason for this is that during the sale and purchase process a lot of decision making is predicated on the quality of the advice and information that buyers and sellers receive. If our clients are getting poor, incomplete, or inaccurate information, bad choices or outcomes may result. This benefits no one in the long run.

Most qualified Realtors will have the breadth of experience to guide you to great recommendations for the following professionals. Here our goal is to provide you with a context for the role each of these professionals play, and some parameters to help you choose them on your own should you need to.

Home Inspector

The home inspector plays one of the most important roles during the purchase process. Their analysis offers a fairly comprehensive assessment of condition of the property (see section on Home Inspections), many times revealing those things that cannot be easily seen during walk-throughs or showings. The home inspector's report is tremendously important to the home-buying decision and sometimes comes up with things that may need to be renegotiated in the contract. Because of this, it is critical to hire someone who is honest, thorough, diligent, and factual. We prefer it to be someone that earns a living from doing home inspections (i.e. does it full-time), and not as a side business. Also, we find it a conflict of interest if the home inspector tries to sell their services as a building contractor as they may not be entirely objective.

When you are deciding on whom to hire as your home inspector, it is important to ask them questions so you have a clear idea of exactly what they do during the inspection (how thorough they are), how much they charge, and what type of report they provide when they complete the job. You may even ask they provide a sample report for you to see along with some references. We strongly advise, when possible, that our clients be present for the inspection if they really want the opportunity to learn about the property first hand. It is a great way to learn and ask questions.

The home inspector should be an individual who will provide a consistent story to both the buyer and seller rather than be overly dramatic to the buyer and understate the situation to the seller. An inspection should be objective. A tile on the roof is either cracked or not, water gets hot or stays cold. By being informative and nonjudgmental, both buyer and seller should feel good about the analysis, especially since it is not uncommon that the inspection may reveal items that need to be repaired or maintained that the seller may not have been aware of previously.

A professional home inspector will have certifications from one or more trade organizations such as:

 National Association of Home Inspectors: ***www.nahi.org***

 Florida Association of Building Inspectors: ***www.fabi.org***

 The American Society of Home Inspectors: ***www.ashi.org***

Mortgage Broker

A mortgage broker is a liaison between borrowers and lenders. They are not the ones to actually loan the money (that is what lenders do), instead they have a relationship with a number of lenders and help to match the needs of each individual client with the best lender for each particular situation.

Mortgage brokers work to gather all the necessary documents, including credit reports, employment verifications, asset disclosures, and appraisals, to complete your file for the lender. It is imperative that you, as the buyer, respond with all the information your mortgage broker requests in a timely manner and are very forthright about all your financial matters. He or she is working on your behalf and can only do the best job with all the information at hand. Further, it is only in your best interest that you know as soon as possible that the financing will all work smoothly. You must be mindful that only within the financing contingency phase of the contract do you have the opportunity to cancel the contract should things not work out.

When you submit your applications to your mortgage broker, they will work to lock in interest rates and loan terms. As we cover in our financing chapter, they will also provide you with the required state and federal disclosures such as the 'Good Faith Estimate' of the associated costs from your lender within a few days of your application. Once an application file is deemed complete, the mortgage broker submits it to the appropriate lender, who then handles loan approval and disbursement.

The mortgage broker is one of the most important parties to the transaction. Lending guidelines and federal requirements have become increasingly more rigorous in the last several years. A good mortgage broker will be very communicative with you and will also be proactive in addressing potential challenges before real issues arise.

Insurance Agent

In Florida when you work with an insurance agent, also known as an insurance broker, they are working on your behalf to find the best coverage available for your circumstances. Like the mortgage broker who works with various lenders, an insurance agent can place a homeowners' policy with various companies.

Most homeowners want to pay the least amount of money and will take the lowest possible coverage. As a consumer, this is not a bad goal. Insurance in the U.S. tends to be more complicated and more expensive than in many countries. Because of our specialization in coastal living, there are a lot of variables that go into the insurance coverage and not a lot of options for insurance companies. To get accurate information the insurance agent may need information from one or more of the other vendors including, appraiser, surveyor, and home inspector. For us, the key work of the insurance agent is to be transparent so that you can determine if your property is effectively insured. It is good to shop around and then have your Realtor help you compare the different options. Most insurance agents try to give you the lowest price possible, which in theory is a good thing. However, they may neglect to discuss the tradeoffs between being less expensive vs. defining how much the actual policy is covering. Your Realtor should be able to help you ask the key questions to determine if the coverage is enough, for example: will it actually be sufficient in the event of the home needing to be rebuilt?

Pest Inspector

The role of the pest inspector is to spend anywhere from twenty minutes to an hour (depending on the size of the property) carefully examining the entire structure of the house, including any access points into the attic or under the house, where pests might be hiding. When they finish, they write up a report showing where they inspected, and any areas that pests may be present. The report may also include information about damage from past infestations, as well as recommendations related to how to prevent pests in the future.

The pest inspector needs to have unquestionable integrity. Most people don't welcome the idea of bugs or creatures living in their home, and knowing this, some pest inspectors may try to sell you more services then are really necessary. Here it is really helpful to use someone who your Realtor or other trusted source can recommend.

We want our readers to be assured that while termites, roaches, rodents and other bugs are part of the ecosystem in Florida and it is not uncommon for problems to arise, there are also solutions that are used every day by these same professionals to deal with them effectively. We ourselves usually only have small issues every few years or so, and are usually able to sort out the problem in the least chemical way possible. There are also companies out there who market themselves as using organic pest control. Again, you want to use a company who is reputable. Many have their own training for their employees and they may also be part of a professional organization such as:

Florida Pest Management Association *www.flpma.org*

Appraiser

The appraiser is an independent third party hired to give a fair and accurate value of the property. If you are working with a lender they will choose the appraiser. If you are paying cash and elect to have an appraisal, you will be able to choose one. You should always choose someone who lives and works in the area and has done hundreds if not thousands of similar appraisals. In our opinion, appraisal is an art rather than a science, and we prefer to see them done by people who have deep familiarity with properties in your neighbourhood. There are subtle as well as major differences that occur, especially with unique properties such as beachfront and waterfront, where there are differences that should be factored in to the value of the property. We receive calls all the time from appraisers looking for comparable data on properties we have listed and sold. We appreciate that they are doing their homework, rather than just relying on internet data.

Always look for an appraiser who holds the **National Association of Realtors General Accredited Appraiser** designation, as this signifies their education and experience to be superior to state requirements.

Escrow Agent

Escrow refers to money held by an independent third party on behalf of two parties who are completing a transaction. When you are purchasing a property and submit your deposit(s), these monies go into escrow. There are three possibilities for who holds escrow (i.e. is the escrow agent) for any given transaction. This is clearly stated in the Contract for Sale or Purchase and is usually chosen by the buyer's Realtor:

1. Real Estate Broker with whom your Realtor is licensed

2. Real Estate Law Firm

3. Title Company

Money held in escrow is not accessible by the buyer or seller during the transaction process, unless and or until the conditions of the contract are met or not. For example: if there is a clause in the contract that says "buyer shall have 10 days to do due diligence", and the buyer decides within the ten days that the property doesn't meet their needs then they will receive a full refund of the deposit as long as they give notice within the ten days that they don't want to proceed. If all terms of the contract are met and the parties get to closing, monies held in escrow will go towards the purchase price of the property.

Tax Accountant

Florida Tax Accountant

We strongly advise all non-resident buyers to invest a few hundred dollars to meet with an accountant in Florida who has a breadth of experience working with international clients. It's important to understand your unique tax situation and make sure you are compliant on all aspects of tax law. In many cases the tax to pay may be zero, but the costs of not filing or defaulting may be much higher.

Tax Accountant in Your Home Country

An international buyer's overall tax liability may be different than that of a U.S. resident, depending upon the buyer's home country's tax treaty with the U.S., if any. Therefore, we also think it is best to consult a tax advisor within your home country that is familiar with the tax treaty. For instance, the capital gains rate for U.S. residents is 15-20 percent (if the property was owned for more than one year). Foreign nationals, however, could be required to pay a higher rate, depending on their home country's tax treaty with the U.S. A tax accountant within your home country, who is familiar with your home country's treaty, would be the best resource for answers to these questions. Please see the tax section further on in this book for more information.

Closing Agent

The closing agent is the person or company who conducts your closing. The closing agent can be one of two things: either a title company, or an attorney. Typically there is not much difference in cost between using a title company or an attorney. The costs for this person or company's services are included in the title insurance fee. In fact around 70 percent of that fee (for properties under $1M) goes to the closing agent and is paid at closing. For properties greater than $1M, the percentage goes down a bit according to the Florida Promulgated Rate Guide. The title company is also the agency that provides the title insurance. Please see the title insurance section for more details on this.

In most counties in Florida, the seller will bear the cost of the title insurance, and subsequently choose the closing agent, though this point may be negotiable in the contract. In Collier, Sarasota, Miami Dade, and Broward counties, the buyer will usually pay for the title insurance and thus normally chooses the agent. **In our opinion, it works in your favor if you choose the closing agent. If you have the opportunity to work this into your contract we would**

recommend doing so. While whomever you choose should technically be neutral for both parties. In our opinion, if you hire a real estate attorney to do the work for you they will not only be more thorough, but will more actively looking out for your interests and advising you.

Title companies will fulfill the requirements of the paperwork for closing; however, their only responsibility really, is to conduct the transaction. Our opinion is that it is better to have someone who will thoroughly search for any potential problems on your behalf, and should they arise, be able to offer legal advice, negotiate, and modify and adjust legal documents and contracts.

Here is a summary of the pros and cons of real estate attorneys vs. title companies as closing agents:

REAL ESTATE ATTORNEY

Pro:	More thorough
Pro:	Offer legal advice, analysis, and guidance (If any problems arise they will likely be able to expeditiously find a solution)
Pro:	Actively looking out for your interests
Pro:	Can modify and extend contracts if closing doesn't go as planned (Even the smoothest anticipated closing can encounter problems)
Con:	Fee included in Title Insurance, though may charge extra fees
Con:	Can overcomplicate

TITLE COMPANY

Pro:	Most closing documents are standard so lawyer not necessary
Pro:	Fee included in title insurance
Con:	Do not give legal advice. (If any problems arise, the title company will push it back to Realtor to resolve)

FINANCING

The first point we want to emphasize is that financing options are available to the global buyer (sometimes also referred to as a 'foreign national'). There are two main choices for global buyers: borrow money with a U.S. lender against the property in Florida, or—if terms for borrowing are more favourable in your home country—leverage real estate assets to borrow against (pulling equity out) to purchase with cash in Florida. Because interest rates are low, many buyers who can pay cash have chosen to finance part of their purchase to leave capital available for subsequent investment opportunities.

Financing Options

CASH

There are benefits to outright cash purchases. For one, your purchase costs are lower as there are lower recording and filing fees, as well as taxes. You have more flexibility in the sense that you do not have to escrow insurance and property taxes. Cash buyers also have a stronger position in the negotiation of the purchase contract. If you are paying cash make sure you consult a currency exchange specialist, as you can potentially achieve far better exchange rates and savings.

That said, there are also many advantages to financing, and many investors may choose not to tie up large amounts of their cash assets in a property purchase.

RE-MORTGAGE IN YOUR HOME COUNTRY (REFINANCING)

If you have equity in your property at home you may be able to release this by re-mortgaging in order to use that equity to buy your Florida home. This is a popular strategy with Canadians and British buyers at the moment, as there are favourable exchange rates, and high prices at home, which mean many people have built up a lot of equity.

GET A MORTGAGE IN YOUR HOME COUNTRY

Many banks will lend buyers up to 80 percent of the purchase price for second homes overseas. This is something to look into if you have a good relationship and long history with your bank.

GET A MORTGAGE IN FLORIDA

Conventional loans in the U.S. generally require a minimum 20 percent equity down payment from U.S. residents. If you decide to obtain financing in the U.S., bear in mind that because of the perceived increased risk in lending to a buyer whose primary residence is outside of the U.S. typically the loans cost a little bit more for global buyer. This cost manifests in two ways: the equity portion required up front is typically greater than 20 percent and may go up to 35 percent. And the interest rate is 0.5 to 2.5 percentage points higher. The reason for this is that currently no secondary market exists where the mortgages can be sold. So the lenders hold those mortgages in their own portfolios for the life of the loan. You can use this mortgage calculator to find out how much your repayments might be *www.martinfunding.com/martin-funding-services/mortgage-tools/.*

Types of U.S. Mortgages

Conventional wisdom is that when interest rates are low, as in our current environment, you lock in those rates for a longer period of time. When interest rates are high, you go for shorter term and adjustable rate options. That said, below are the most common mortgage programs.

FIXED RATE MORTGAGES

A fixed rate mortgage has traditionally been the most popular type of mortgage in Florida. This is a mortgage in which the interest rate stays constant for the duration of the loan. With a fixed rate mortgage, you pay both capital and interest over a fixed period of (usually) 15, 20 or 30 years at exactly the same monthly payment for the duration of the loan. This type of mortgage suits buyers who value knowing exactly what their repayments are going to be over the long term, and don't want to take any risk of being affected by rising interest rates.

Generally, with shorter length loans, the interest rate is lower. On a longer-term loan your interest rate is higher but your monthly payment is lower compared to a shorter length loan. A long-term loan is more suitable for persons who have a limited budget and need their monthly house payment to be the least amount possible. The advantage of a short-term loan is being able to pay your loan off more quickly, in effect reducing the amount of total interest paid throughout the duration of your loan.

ADJUSTABLE RATE MORTGAGES

Adjustable rate mortgages (ARM) are loans in which the

interest rate changes based on the market interest rate. With an ARM there is usually a fixed interest rate for the start of the loan (typically one to seven years depending on your deal) after which, the rate is adjusted either once or twice a year (depending on the mortgage type) and will fluctuate in line with independent published financial indexes.

Adjustable rate mortgages (ARM) to begin with come with rates lower than a fixed rate mortgage but will rise and fall over time depending on the market. People like the ARM option because it can mean savings, however it is also mean unexpected changes in monthly payments. Its lower initial rate may help you qualify for a larger mortgage amount. ARM mortgages have an adjustable "cap" which limits how much the interest can go up or down. This helps prevent big surprise increases in your monthly payment. If you know your income is rising and will keep pace with an ARM's adjustments, or you plan to sell in a few years, this could be a good choice.

BALLOON MORTGAGES

Balloon mortgages are short-term mortgages where lower regular payments are made until the end of the loan term, when a final larger payment is due. This is useful when you know you don't want to be tied down to a mortgage for a long time and that you will be able to come up with a large sum of money not too far in the future.

The advantage of this type of loan is that the interest rate on balloon loans is generally lower than a 15 or 30 year mortgage, which means lower monthly payments. The disadvantage is that at the end of the term you will have to come up with a lump sum of money to pay off your lender.

INTEREST-ONLY MORTGAGE TYPES

With an interest only mortgage you only pay the interest due. The total borrowed amount is due at the end of the loan term. This offers the lowest possible payment without actually increasing the owed amount owed.

COMBO / PIGGYBACK MORTGAGE LOAN TYPES

This financing consists of two loans: a first and second mortgage. The mortgages can be fixed rate or adjustable-rate or a combination of the two. When the down payment is less than 20 percent, borrowers take out two loans to avoid having to pay private mortgage insurance.

EQUITY MORTGAGE LOAN (HOME EQUITY LINE OF CREDIT)

These are junior to and second in position to, the existing mortgage. Borrowers take out an equity loan to receive cash against their house. The loans can be any type: adjustable, fixed, or credit which the borrower can draw funds from as and when needed.

There are financing options for global buyers for almost any situation, and once the right mortgage broker

understands your circumstances, he or she will help you find the right fit for your specific needs. Your Realtor should have good relationships with mortgage brokers and lenders who can help you achieve your financing aims.

Estimate of Financing Costs

If you apply for financing in the U.S., by federal law your lender is required to provide you with a statement called a 'Good Faith Estimate' of the associated costs within a few days of your application. This is a standardized document used to detail all the costs of obtaining your mortgage, including both monthly and one-off payments. Usually these are between 1-3 percent of the transaction value. Just before the actual closing, all these costs are documented on the Settlement Statement (HUD1 Form) as mentioned above. You also can use this handy calculator to estimate your closing costs during your property search: ***www.facc.firstam.com/***

Buyers' Quick Reference Cost Guide

Please see the appendix for an example of a closing statement illustrating the itemization of all costs, also known as a Settlement Statement or HUD-1.

Title Charge

- ✔ Title Insurance
- ✔ Settlement or closing fee
- ✔ Document preparation
- ✔ Attorney's fees

Additional Settlement Charges:

- ✔ Homeowner's Insurance
- ✔ Appraisal Fee (optional for cash buyers)
- ✔ Prepaid property taxes or utility bills – The seller will receive a credit from the buyer on the closing statement for any prepaid property taxes or utilities.

Items Payable In Connection With Loan:

- ✔ Loan Origination Fee
- ✔ Loan Discount
- ✔ Credit Report

Additional Items Required By Lender To Be Paid In Advance

- ✔ Interest
- ✔ Mortgage Insurance Premium

Prepaid Expenses Held in Escrow

- ✔ Homeowner's insurance
- ✔ Local property taxes

AUTHOR'S NOTE

When you take out a mortgage, the mortgage company may establish an escrow account under the terms of the mortgage, to ensure the insurance and property taxes on the property get paid during the loan term. So rather than just collecting the mortgage payment each month, the mortgage company will also collect an amount to cover taxes and insurance. They are then responsible for the accounting of this separate escrow account, and for submitting the taxes and insurance payments in a timely fashion. In these cases the lender will collect an amount of future costs via the closing agent.

3

CHAPTER

OWNING A
FLORIDA
HOME

REAL ESTATE TAXES

There are three types of taxes relating to real estate. First, all properties in Florida are assessed a taxable value and owners pay an annual **property tax** based on this value (except churches, schools, government entities). This tax is paid to the local municipality.

Second, if you sell your home, there may be a **capital gains tax** on the profit realized from the sale. For this scenario, there are federal guidelines set forth for global buyers under the **Foreign Investment in Real Property Tax Act (FIRPTA).**

The third tax category only applies to rental properties. If there is net profit on the rental income, there may be a **federal tax on the profit generated from renting out a**

vacation home or other investment property. In addition, for short-term rentals there is a **sales tax** which is generally charged to the renter and submitted to the local government. We will explain the tax considerations for rentals more fully in our section on property rentals.

As we've mentioned before, tax law is an area where we would advocate using a professional to make sure you know how taxes may apply to your specific situation. It's one of the most important things to understand when buying real estate in another country, as the tax costs could drastically affect your predicted return. It costs around $300 for a meeting with a tax expert and we think it is money well spent, as they'll be able to advise you on your unique situation, and make sure you are compliant in all areas.

In this section we will discuss property tax, since it is applicable to all property owners on a recurring annual basis. We will introduce you to FIRPTA so that you are aware of it for your future tax planning purposes, especially since it is an important topic to discuss with your tax advisor in your initial meeting. For further details on FIRPTA please refer to our chapter on Selling your Florida Property.

Property Tax

In Florida, property taxes go towards public schools and infrastructure, including roads, libraries, and medical services. The local county property appraiser sets the assessed value (based on market data of prior calendar year) to your property as of January first each year. The Florida statutes direct how each county determines property values. That value is published/released around late summer each year. Each county has its own website defining the process for its residents, so you can look this up for your particular location.

Property taxes are not due until March first. However, you can begin to pay from the first of November of the tax year. For each month that you pay in advance (for a total of four months) you receive a one percent discount on your total tax bill (for a maximum total discount of four percent). For example, if your property tax is $4000, by paying in November you save $160. If you do decide to make Florida your primary residence, you will be entitled to a slight reduction (up to $50,000) in the assessed value of your property, thereby reducing your property tax, through something called the Homestead Exemption.

Foreign Investment in Real Property Tax Act (FIRPTA)

(Please see the future chapter on Selling Your Home, for further detailed discussion of FIRTPA)

Like many countries, one of the ways the U.S. Government generates its income is by taxing the profits on the sale of real estate investments made within the country. This is a type of capital gains tax, which applies to citizens and non-citizens alike, who sell investment property (the sale of a primary residence is handled differently). U.S. citizens are subject to this tax as part of their regular income tax. For global buyers, FIRPTA is the tax law that sets the parameters for handling the payment of taxes for foreign persons who sell U.S. real estate interests.

Where FIRPTA comes into play is on investment properties which are sold at over $300,000 and which have appreciated in value. Effectively you are paying tax on the profit you've made on the property. The rules for withholding can be cumbersome to understand, so it's advisable as always, to take legal or accountancy advice to make sure you comply. As always, it's better to spend the money up front to make clear what you need to do, rather than deal with any unintended consequences from simply not knowing how it works.

UTILITIES

In the United States we use the term **utilities** to refer to the services consumers use in residential and commercial settings: electricity, natural gas, water/sewer, TV, internet, and telephone services. To establish any of these services, you'll need to contact the local utility companies and set up an account. In contrast to some other countries, where there is competition for many types of utilities, in Florida there may be only one or two options for a given service. You will most likely deal with separate companies for electric, gas, and water/sewer. For television you can elect between cable, satellite and fibre optic. Internet is available either through a cable television company or the telephone company.

Depending on where your property is in Florida, the company that provides your services may be administered by the municipality, a private company with government oversight, or an independent private company. Whichever utilities you elect to have, you can expect to get charged month-to-month for the utilities used. When you set up your account, some companies will require new clients to pay a one-time deposit to secure the account. Generally this deposit is returned after a certain period of time or after you close your account. For one of our recent buyers from Germany the deposit taken was around $500 dollars. The utilities company may also perform an international credit check, or ask for references before agreeing to set you up with an account.

These days probably the most efficient way of dealing with energy bills is through email. Most companies will now bill by email, and the consumer simply pays the bill online at the energy company's website. Like many other businesses today, most Florida utility companies will permit you to set up automatic payments that will withdraw your payments from a checking account. Because many utility bills aren't a fixed expense, some people are hesitant to set up automatic payments, but it will help you prevent late fees and make the bill paying process simpler. Many utility companies also offer the option of paying their bills via credit card. Some consumers like this option as it can add miles or points towards their frequent flyer programs.

Electric

There is only one energy provider for any given area within Florida. Unlike in some European countries, there is still limited use of renewable energy in the state. To learn about energy saving measures, most electric companies in Florida have a program where your home can be energy tested and recommendations can be made as to what steps you can take to consume less energy. Sometimes they will also provide rebates that offer significant savings or incentives for customers to install or retrofit their homes with more energy saving measures such as appliances, windows, or insulation.

Propane and Natural Gas

Some properties use propane gas which is delivered by truck on a regular basis to a tank that is either above or below ground. This is generally used to heat swimming pools. In our experience this is a more expensive fuel than natural gas, but it may be the only option.

Natural gas is available in some areas and it is relatively inexpensive. Many homes actually potentially have access to natural gas; however the current owner may not yet have run the line from the street to the house. That generally, is an owner's expense; however, in our experience if you are going to have two or more gas appliances, the gas company will pay for the cost of installing the line from the street and set up the metre at your house. Homeowners may elect to use natural gas for just the pool water heater and an outdoor grill, or also include one or more of the indoor appliances such as the fireplace, stove, clothes dryer, and/or house hot water heater.

We want to share that should a tenant choose not to pay their rent, the procedures in Florida are very well documented. Thus, if you are in a situation that you need to remove a tenant it is an easier process than you may have experienced in other countries.

Water/Sewerage

Water consumed in Florida is sourced from underground aquifers as well as lakes and rivers. Each month the metre on your property will be read to track consumption. If your home uses a septic tank, sewerage will not be applicable, but if you do have a sewerage service it will typically be billed through your water provider as a percentage of total water consumed.

Television

When you are shopping for how to get TV into your home, there is usually a choice between cable, satellite and fibre optic. In Florida, most TV is delivered to homes via cable, and there are usually a variety of plans and packages available through one local cable company. The cable company may offer to bundle together phone/internet and TV packages into one lower monthly payment. The local phone company can also bundle these three services. If you elect to use satellite you may have a couple of companies to choose from. It is not uncommon for promotions to be offered from any of these providers as there is healthy competition in this area.

Internet

As with TV, usually you have a few options for internet: cable, fibre optic, or DSL broadband. Once you have a connection set up you can buy a wireless router (usually available from your provider) and then you are free to use WIFI anywhere in your home. Unlike in some European countries, you don't have to have a landline to get Internet connection. It can be provided from any communications company or via a cable company, and can also be provided independent of TV and phone service.

Waste Collection/Recycling Services

The municipality almost always handles waste collection and recycling. For most areas, the waste will be collected once or twice a week, and usually the cost of pick up is included in property taxes. While the municipality may choose to outsource the waste collection to a private company, the billing will still be included in your property taxes. This is true even in private or gated communities.

In condos or apartments the situation is slightly different when it comes to waste and rubbish collection. Usually the association of the building will organize this service, though you may get charged a fee for this. Usually your responsibility is only to get the rubbish to the collection spot, or often to simply drop it in a rubbish chute. Condos and apartments tend to have strict rules about the ways waste is handled, as it is obviously really important from a pest, and health and safety perspective for the entire building and all the residents, that waste is disposed of efficiently and hygienically.

BANKING IN FLORIDA

In our experience, if you own property in Florida and/or plan to spend time in the U.S. on a regular basis, you may find it easier to have a U.S. bank account. Whether to pay bills on your real estate, for the ease and low cost of withdrawing cash from a local ATM, or the simplicity of paying for goods and services, we feel that having a Florida bank account is practical. Opening an account is a fairly straightforward process. After opening the account, because of online or mobile banking, you may not need to use a physical branch going forward.

At the time of printing of this book, we consulted a large multi-national bank, a very prominent U.S. bank, and a

Florida regional bank about how a non-resident can establish a bank account. The requirements to open an account at any one of these three banks were fairly straightforward. You must appear in person to the local branch with a passport and a secondary ID (consult the bank for what qualifies as generally there are a number of options). In some cases there may be a minimum amount of money that you must deposit initially.

We recently had two sets of global clients open accounts with regional banks in our area. Both were easy and straightforward. One bank did not require a large deposit, just that but there always be a minimum of $500 in the account. The other did require a deposit of $10,000 and the clients' passport.

Every bank will vary in its requirements, and will differ in the services, charges and facilities it offers to international clients. It's worth shopping around all the major banks, both in your home country and in Florida, to find the best solution for your needs.

United States Brokerage Accounts

One of the biggest differences between a bank account and a brokerage account in the United States is that with a brokerage account you can buy and sell shares of your favorite company stocks, like Apple, Google, General Electric, etc. However, it is much easier to open a bank account than a brokerage account. A combination of U.S. laws and bank policies create an unclear path to opening an account. While you do not have to be a US Citizen to open an account, you do have to be a resident. It seems, however, that there is no standard definition from the brokerage community as to what constitutes residency. Brokerages are looking at new accounts for non-U.S. citizens on a case by case basis. Our suggestion is to get recommendations from your Florida based team of advisors such as your Realtor, lawyer, accountant, neighbours, etc. Then do some internet research and call your favourites to determine your eligibility. By contacting your choices directly and explaining your individual situation, you and the brokerage can then work together to determine if and how they can open an account for you. The good news is that once you have an account (similar to your bank account) you will be able to access it 24 hours a day, seven days a week as long as you can access the internet. The world of finance never sleeps.

Moving Money Internationally

PAYPAL

PayPal is a global internet payment site which allows for payments and money transfers to be made between individuals anywhere in the world. PayPal charges fees per transaction. These fees may be based on the currency used, whether payments are made through credit card or directly from a bank account, the country of the sender, the country of the recipient, the amount sent and the recipient's account type. In our experience, PayPal's transactional fees are quite low in comparison to what you might be charged by your bank for international wire transfer. However, their exchange rate is not particularly favourable. So it is worth checking if, once a better exchange rate is factored in, it's cheaper to transfer the money with your bank.

WIRE TRANSFER

A wire transfer is an electronic funds transfer from one individual or institution's bank account to another. Most banks nowadays have facilities to easily wire money internationally. While this probably won't be a good day-to-day solution, as fixed fees are often incurred, it can be the most secure and efficient way of transferring large sums of money at one time. Most services can have the money in the U.S. receiver's bank account in two to three days. For many bank accounts, once you have set up an international receiver with details such as their international bank identifier number (IBAN) or SWIFT CODE, it's then possible to make automatic international payments to those receivers using your bank's website, or even your phone app.

CREDIT/DEBIT CARDS

VISA and MasterCard credit and debit cards will work throughout Florida at ATMs and in most restaurants and shops. American Express is slightly less widely accepted. Credit card companies, especially the larger banks, tend to offer very good exchange rates. Having a credit card that does not charge an international transaction fee potentially offers a very competitive way to spend or move money abroad. There are many cards available with different benefits catering to international clients.

IMMIGRATION: ENTERING THE U.S.

Before we dive into the riveting topic of immigration and visas, we want to provide some commentary and context. First, we would like to make it clear for our readers: to own real estate in Florida you do not need any special documentation. If you can get your money into the U.S., you can invest. Second, if your aim is to spend time in Florida enjoying the sun, sea, and mild winters, you can expect three months (the time period most visitors are initially approved for) to go by very quickly. This is why we find many global buyers opting for the six month temporary visa so that they can settle in longer and/or visit more often and enjoy the Florida lifestyle and climate. Third, a very popular strategy for many global buyers looking to move their families to the U.S., whether for financial, educational, safety, or environmental reasons, is to take the route of the EB-5 Investment Visa. With these keys points in mind, we bring you the highlights on U.S. immigration.

Visas Overview

A citizen of a foreign country who wishes to enter the U.S. must generally obtain a visa granting entry—a travel document that is affixed to one's passport. The intended purpose of the travel, along with other factors, determine what type of visa is required under U.S. immigration law. As we elaborate on below, visitors from certain countries who wish to come for a period of less than 90 days do not need to obtain a visa. If your country of origin does not fall within this category, or you intend to stay beyond 90 days, you will need to obtain a temporary visa. If your objective is to live or work in the U.S. there are two main routes to go:

1. Apply for one of the permanent residency visas (also called "immigrant visas" or "Green Cards") or

2. Apply for one of the temporary residency visas (also called "nonimmigrant visas").

People have been immigrating to U.S. for hundreds of years. In fact 2013 marked the 500th anniversary of the Spanish explorer Juan Ponce de León's landing in St Augustine, Florida (please see our market summary for this historical and charming town) when he claimed the region for the Spanish crown. According to the U.S. Department of State, there are 65 million visitors to the U.S. each year. Nowadays, the process for applying for the many types of visas is quite straightforward. However, **if your aim is to obtain a longer term or permanent residency visa, we feel it really pays to find an immigration attorney who has processed hundreds of applications. With their experience and understanding of the nuances and subtleties of the process, they will likely be able to really advise you on the option that offers the greatest chance of successful approval, as well as save you much time and money going through the process.** To illustrate a bit further: one popular option for establishing residency is the EB-5 Investment Visa. There are minimum guidelines that the U.S. will expect you to achieve, however a professional will know if they are more or less stringent depending on prevailing economic conditions or other factors, and will likely be able to guide you more effectively.

Those who want to spend extended periods visiting the U.S .may apply for a tourist visa extending their stay up to six months. If you choose to seek employment or start a business in the U.S. there is a category of working visas. And finally, if you desire to be in the U.S. long-term, you may choose to apply for permanent resident status (Green Card) and eventually citizenship. Below is a summary of the main visa types that are relevant to buyers of Florida property, and the criteria to qualify. Our purpose in this section is to provide an orientation, however these programs are always subject to change so we recommend you always get the latest information at *www.travel.state.gov/visa/*

Visa Waiver

The Visa Waiver Program allows visitors from thirty-seven countries to visit the U.S. for a period of 90 days or less without a visa, as long as they meet all the criteria specified. Here is a chart to see which countries qualify:

Andorra	Hungary	New Zealand
Australia	Iceland	Norway
Austria	Ireland	Portugal
Belgium	Italy	San Marino
Brunei	Japan	Singapore
Czech Republic	Latvia	Slovakia
Denmark	Liechtenstein	Slovenia
Estonia	Lithuania	South Korea

Finland	Luxembourg	Spain
France	Malta	Sweden
Germany	Monaco	Switzerland
Greece	The Netherlands	Taiwan
		United Kingdom

*Source: www.travel.state.gov/visa/temp/without/
without_1990.html*

All travellers who are eligible for the Visa Waiver Program are required to be authorized through the Electronic System for Travel Authorization (ESTA) before departing for the U.S.

Temporary Visas

For those who wish to remain in the U.S. temporarily, or for those who wish to enter temporarily before applying for more permanent status.

- B-1/B-2 Visitor Visas, which permit a visitor to remain in the U.S. for up to six months (employment is not permitted)

- F-1 Student Visas, which permit foreign students to attend U.S. educational institutions. Limited employment is permitted in some cases

- J-1 Visas for Participants in Exchange Programs, which permit business trainees to come to the U.S. to learn about an occupation or profession for up to 18 months

- K-1 Visas for a Fiancé (e) of a U.S. citizen

- K-3 Visas for a Spouse of a U.S. citizen

- P-1 Visas for Internationally Recognized Entertainment Groups and Athletes.

Working Visas

If you would like to work in the U.S. temporarily, you will need a specific visa based on the purpose of your travel and type of work you will be doing. In order to obtain a visa, you will need to meet specific requirements to qualify for a temporary work visa under immigration law. The consular officer will determine whether you qualify for the visa.

In addition, your prospective employer must generally file a nonimmigrant petition on your behalf with USCIS (U.S. Citizen and Immigration Services). U.S. companies must file Form we-129, Petition for Nonimmigrant Worker, with United States Citizenship and Immigration Services (USCIS), Department of Homeland Security (DHS).

- E-2 Treaty Investor Visas, which permit investors from certain countries to invest a substantial amount of money and acquire a controlling interest in an active U.S. business. The visa is issued for up to five years and is renewable. The investor can work in his or her own business. The spouse can qualify for an unrestricted temporary work card. Children up to the age of 21 can accompany the parents and attend school, but cannot work

- H-1B Visas for Workers in Specialty Occupations, which permit employment of professional level workers by a sponsoring employer. The visa is issued for up to three years and can be renewed another three years (additional renewals are possible in some cases)

- R-1 Visas for Religious Workers who are being transferred to the U.S. by a related international church

- TN Visas for certain professional workers from Mexico and Canada. This visa is issued for one year and can be renewed in one-year increments

- L-1 Visas for Multinational Managers, Executives and Specialized Knowledge employees who are being transferred to the U.S. by a related international company

- O-1 Visas for Aliens with Extraordinary Ability who are seeking temporary employment. This visa is issued for up to three years and can be renewed in one-year increments.

Long-term Visas

It is possible to become a permanent resident (Green Card holder) of the United States through a job or offer of employment. However, some categories require a certification from the U.S. Department of Labor to show that there are not enough U.S. workers who are able, willing, qualified, and available in the geographic area where the immigrant is to be employed, and that no American workers are displaced by foreign workers.

- EB-1: for aliens with extraordinary ability, outstanding professors and researchers, or multinational business managers and executives

- EB-2: for aliens with exceptional ability or aliens with advanced degrees (employer/sponsor required)

- EB-3: for professional workers (with university degree), skilled workers and unskilled workers (employer/ sponsor required)

- EB-4: for religious workers

- EB-5: for aliens who invest $1 million and create 10 new full time jobs (in limited situations, an investment of $500,000 and the creation of five new jobs is acceptable).

EB-5 Investment Visa

This program permits the EB-5 Investor and his or her spouse and unmarried children under age 21 to become Lawful Permanent Residents of the U.S. (i.e., obtain "Green Card" status).

TO QUALIFY, EB-5 INVESTORS MUST MEET 3 REQUIREMENTS:

1. Make an investment of least $500,000 or $1,000,000 in a pooled investment vehicle

2. Provide detailed evidence showing that the money invested was legitimately earned and

3. Their investment must cause the creation of 10 new jobs in the U.S.

EB-5 investors first apply for a Green Card using Form

we-526 with supporting evidence explaining the investment project and the source of the money invested. Once Form we-526 is approved, EB-5 investors obtain a temporary two year conditional Green Card. At the end of the two year conditional Green Card, EB-5 investors must file a second application with USCIS to prove that they remain invested in their project, and that their investment actually created the 10 new jobs required.

The program has a total of 10,000 EB-5 visas available each year. No waiting lists exist at present. Most EB-5 investors originate from China.

Citizenship

Once you have held a Green Card for ten years, and fulfilled all the necessary tax requirements, you are eligible to apply for citizenship.

SCHOOLS AND UNIVERSITIES

For us, one of the most interesting trends in education today is the sheer number of international students who come to the U.S. for school. This influences and relates to the real estate market in a few ways. First, parents may decide that instead of paying to rent housing for four years while their child is in university, they can buy a house or condo for the young adult to live in. If it is large enough, they might even take on a roommate or two and collect rental income, while also potentially holding an appreciating asset. Even after the child(ren) graduate, it could become an ongoing source of income. In some cases, the entire family moves with their student(s) to live in the U.S. while the child(ren) attend school. Thus, in the areas that have schools, colleges, and universities the market demand for single family homes is very steady. Another really compelling real estate opportunity in university towns is that of investing in rental properties which cater to students, as there is consistent demand for rental housing.

The American education system, particularly its university system, is known to be among the best in the world, and many people want their children and grandchildren to be educated in the U.S. While there are good schools and universities all over the country, not all areas of the country offer families the tropical weather and lifestyle that Florida does!!

Each year roughly 33,000 international students attend university in Florida. In terms of higher educational institutions, Florida has over 57 colleges or universities. For primary or high school age kids, options range from sending your child to boarding school to relocating the family and attending a state/public school, or private day school. Families from around the world also enroll their child athletes in several specialized sports training programs here in Florida.

Boarding Schools

One way of increasing the odds that your child is admitted to a U.S. college of their choice may be to send them to secondary school in America. Boarding schools (where children live at school during term time) cater to international students.

Traditionally, boarding schools in the U.S. have been concentrated on the Eastern seaboard, with some renowned and historical academies and colleges populating the New England states. However, in recent history many international families have chosen to send their children to study in Florida, and at last count there are ten boarding schools in the state. Admiral Farragut Academy in St. Augustine, as an example, counts students from 24 countries on its role.

For most boarding schools that accept International Students, a certain level of English is usually required for admission. Most schools thus usually require a foundation year in English, or an intensive English summer class if the student can't demonstrate a certain required level of proficiency.

Here is a list of Florida's Boarding Schools:

SCHOOL	GRADES	# OF INTER-NATIONAL STUDENTS	CITY
The Bolles School	K-12	90	Jacksonville
Florida Air Academy	6-12	200	Melbourne
IMG Academy	5-12	600	Bradenton
Lake Mary Preparatory	6-12	125	Lake Mary
Montverde Academy	7-12	300	Montverde
North Broward Preparatory School	6-12	200	Coconut Creek
Saddlebrook Academy	6-12	50	Tampa
Saint Andrew's School	9-12	100	Boca Raton
Windermere Academy	6-12	200	Windermere

Student Visas

Student Visas for University

Once a prospective student is admitted to a college or university and has demonstrated the ability to finance their education, the admissions office will send them a Form I-20. They are to take the I-20 form, along with their acceptance letter, passport and copies of sponsorship letters and bank statements to prove financial support, to the United States embassy or consulate nearest their home. There they will complete a preliminary application for the visa. Once they have acquired the visa stamp in their passport, they are ready to enter the U.S.

Student Visas for State/Public Primary or High School in the U.S.

For most students whose main purpose for being in the U.S. is education, the F1 visa is applicable. However, this visa places a lot of restrictions on access to state/public schooling.

- Students cannot get this visa in order to study in primary/elementary school, only in secondary/high school

- Students attending public high school on an F1 visa must reimburse the school for the full cost of tuition

- The student can only attend for 12 months on an F1 visa.

This visa often applies when a child is being sent to stay with a relative in the U.S. in order to study.

If the student's parents have the correct non-immigrant visa or Green Card and are present in the U.S., their dependent children can attend public/state school. Examples of non-immigrant visas which allow your children to qualify for public/state school include:

- Investment Visas

- Working Visas

- Athlete Visas

- Artist Visas

- Specialty Occupation Workers

- Intra-company transferees

- Workers with extraordinary abilities

Student Visas for Private School

For your child to attend private school in the U.S., you must also obtain an F1 visa. In this case there are not so many restrictions on the visa. So as long as you are paying for the schooling the child can attend, regardless of his or her parents' immigration status or visa. In order to apply for the visa your chosen school will give you an I-20 form showing that your child is registered with the school. Not all schools can issue these I-20 forms, so you need to check your chosen school is eligible.

GETTING MEDICAL CARE IN FLORIDA

Obviously, in order to maximize the enjoyment of your stay in Florida, it is best to stay healthy. However, should you need access to medical care, doctors, clinics, and hospitals are very accessible in Florida. There are over 45,000 doctors in the state. As with everything, we encourage you to ask your Realtor, friends, and neighbours for recommendations for the type of care provider you need.

Health care in the U.S. is not free—however, it does not need to be expensive. Most places you go will ask to have full payment or proof of insurance and any co-pay (please see the glossary for a definition of a co-pay) at the time of your visit. If you opt to pay out of your own pocket, you usually can use cash, credit card, or cheque from a U.S. bank (if you have already set up an account). If you have health insurance, you may still need to pay for services (perhaps either the full or reduced fee) at the time of your medical visit, then get reimbursed a partial or full refund at a later date from your insurance company.

WALK-IN CLINICS

In addition to doctor's offices and hospitals, there is an extensive network of walk-in clinics (also known as Urgent Care) throughout Florida. **Walk-in clinics are set up to handle non life-threatening injuries, illnesses and accidents and do not require an appointment. Many are open seven days a week and for 10-12 hours per day, making them very convenient and accessible.** To find these you simply need to do an Internet search for "walk in clinics (insert your location)" and you will usually have several choices. Walk-in clinics may be a very viable option for unexpected healthcare needs during your time in Florida and should be more reasonably priced, especially for those who are not filing insurance and instead paying up front with cash, credit card, or cheque.

Many global visitors and property owners have a lot of options for health care coverage during their travel from their home country. Each person's situation and options vary according to their country of origin, age, length of stay/ stays in Florida. For those who are holidaying on a short-term basis, most travel insurance from your home country will be adequate to cover you for your trip. These health reimbursement policies may be part of a homeowner's insurance policy, part of a credit card policy, and/or part of the state-sponsored program in the respective home country.

The great news is that if your home country does not provide the best solution for your needs, short-term health insurance is available at very reasonable rates from numerous global companies. Many of these also include a travel component covering the transportation and accommodation costs of your trip should you have to cancel for reasons such as illness. For example, a quote from one website for a German (under age 66) traveling to the U.S. for up to six months was about $125/month. A couple traveling together would be roughly $105/month for each person. For a family of four is about $66/month per person. This was for very comprehensive coverage.

Once you are a property owner in Florida and plan to stay for longer periods, it may be preferable to specifically research another type of coverage. There are numerous global providers with a myriad of programs. It seems that the options begin to diminish for visitors over 70. If this applies to you, it would be wise to take the time to thoroughly consider the options available to you in advance of any long-term stays.

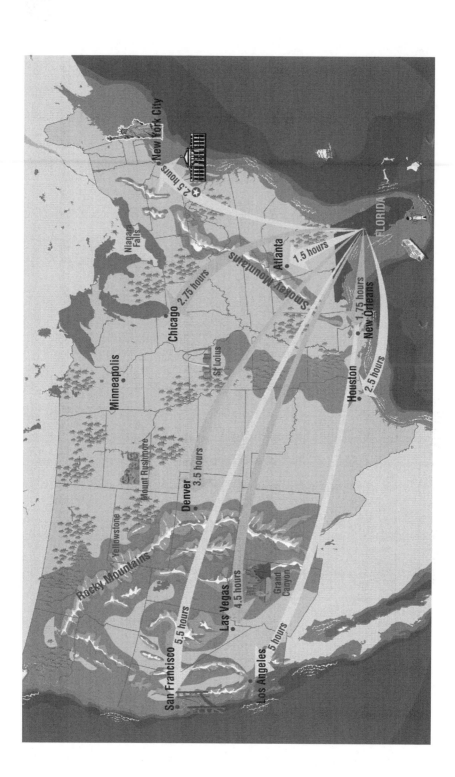

FLIGHTS TO AND FROM FLORIDA

One of the things we are asked when talking to people about Florida is: "Is it easy to get to?" With the increased desirability of Florida, airlines have been continuously adding flights and destinations. It is both easy to enter and leave the United States from Florida, and also easy to fly directly to hundreds of destinations in the U.S. including: San Francisco, Chicago, New York, Las Vegas, Los Angeles and Boston. So many people think only of Miami or Orlando when they first consider Florida. As we tried to illustrate in the chapter highlighting the various regions throughout the state, there is actually SO much more to see and do than most initially believe.

We bring you this section about Florida's international airports, as well as what international routes the airlines service, to illustrate the flight accessibility into the various regions of Florida. The great news is once you land at any given airport within the state, there are a myriad of wonderful destinations that you probably have yet to discover within one or two hours drive. We would encourage you to look at all the possibilities when you consider visiting or living in Florida.

Florida has a total of 15 international airports! That accounts for a LOT of flights in and out of the country from the Sunshine State: in terms of foreign cities served that is 133 in all! There are 24 flight routes to/from cities in Canada, 32 routes to/from of Europe, 38 routes to/from South America, 20 routes to/from Central America, eight routes to/from Mexico, and 71 routes to/from the Bahamas and Caribbean.

Here is a detailed list of the direct international flight routes to/from Florida airports as of the printing of this book:

CANADA
Edmonton, Calgary, Winnipeg, Toronto, London, Ottawa, Hamilton, Montreal, Quebec, Moncton, Halifax, St. John's

CARIBBEAN & BAHAMAS
Marsh Harbour, Nassau, Santo Domingo, Port of Spain, Aruba, Kingston, Montego Bay

CENTRAL AMERICA
San Salvador, San Jose, Costa Rica, Panama City

ORLANDO AIRPORT TO / FROM

MEXICO
Cancun, Mexico City

EUROPE
Belfast, Dublin, Cardiff, London, Birmingham, Frankfurt, Manchester, Glasgow, Oslo

SOUTH AMERICA
Bogota, San Paulo, Rio de Janiero

MEXICO
Cancun,
Toluca

CENTRAL AMERICA
Guatemala City, Guatemala,
Managua, Nicaragua, Panama
City, Panama, San Jose, Costa Rica,
San Pedro Sula, Honduras, San
Salvador, El Salvador

**FT. LAUDERDALE
AIRPORT TO/FROM**

CANADA
Montreal, Ottawa,
Quebec, Toronto

SOUTH AMERICA
Armenia, Colombia,
Bogota, Colombia, Cartagena,
Colombia, Medellin,
Colombia, Lima, Peru

EUROPE
Copenhagen,
Denmark, Frankfurt,
Germany, Oslo, Norway,
Stockholm, Sweden

CARIBBEAN & BAHAMAS
Bimini, Bahamas, Cap Haitien, Haiti,
Freeport, Bahamas, George Town, Bahamas,
Govenor'sHarbour, Bahamas, Guantanamo Bay, Cuba,
Kingston, Jamaica, Montego Bay, Jamaica, Marsh
Harbour, Bahamas, Nassau, Bahamas, North Eleuthra,
Bahamas, Oranjestad, Aruba, Port au Prince, Haiti, Port of
Spain, Trinidad, Punta Cana, Dominican Republic, Santa
Domingo, Dominican Republic, Santiago, Dominican
Republic, San Salvador, Bahamas, St. Marrten, St.
Marrten, Treasure Cay, Bahamas

ORLANDO-SANFORD
AIRPORT TO/FROM

BRAZIL
Brasilia, Porto
Alegre, Rio de
Janeiro, Sao Paulo

EUROPE
Amsterdam,
Netherlands
Reykjavik, Iceland

PALM BEACH
AIRPORT TO/FROM

BAHAMAS
Marsh Harbour

CANADA
Montreal
Toronto

MIAMI AIRPORT TO/FROM

MEXICO
Cancun, Cozumel, Merida, Mexico City

CENTRAL AMERICA
Belize City, Belize, Guatemala City, Guatemala, Liberia, Costa Rica, Managua, Nicaragua, Panama City, Panama, Roatan, Honduras, San Jose, Costa Rica, San Pedro Sula, Honduras, San Salvador, El Salvador, Tegucigalpa, Honduras

CARIBBEAN & BAHAMAS
Antigua, West Indies, Aruba, Netherland Antilles, Barbados, West Indies, Bonaire, Netherland Antilles, Bermuda, Cap Haitien, Haiti, Cayman Brac, West Indies, Curacao, Netherland Antilles, Fort de France, Martinique, Freeport, Bahamas, George Town, Bahamas, Grand Cayman, West Indies, Grenada, Windward Islands, Kingston, Jamaica, La Romana, Dominican Republic, Marsh Harbour, Bahamas, Montego Bay, Jamaica, Nassau, Bahamas, North Eleuthera, Bahamas, Pointe a Pitre, Guadeloupe, Port Au Prince, Haiti, Port of Spain, Trinidad & Tobago, Providenciales, Turks & Caicos, Puerto Plata, Dominican Republic, Punta Cana, Dominican Republic, San Juan, Puerto Rico, Santiago, Dominican Republic, Santo Domingo, Dominican Republic, St. Croix, Virgin Islands, St. Kitts, Leeward Islands, St. Lucia, West Indies, St. Maarten, Netherlands Antilles, St. Thomas, Virgin Islands

MIAMI AIRPORT TO/FROM

EUROPE
Amsterdam, Netherlands, Barcelona, Spain, Berlin, Germany, Dusseldorf, Germany, Frankfurt, Germany, Lisbon, Portugal, London, England, Madrid, Spain, Milan, Italy, Moscow (Domodedevo), Russia, Moscow (Sheremetyevo), Russia, Paris (Charles de Gaulle), Rome, Italy, Zurich, Switzerland

CANADA
Calgary,, Montreal, Quebec, Toronto, Ontario

SOUTH AMERICA
Asuncion, Paraguay, Barcelona, Venezuela, Barranquilla, Colombia, Belo Horizonte, Brazil, Bogota, Colombia, Brasilia, Brazil, Buenos Aires, Argentina, Cali, Colombia, Caracas, Venezuela, Cartagena, Colombia, Curitiba, Brazil, Georgetown, Guyana, Guayaquil, Ecuador, La Paz, Bolivia, Lima, Peru, Manaus, Brazil, Maracaibo, Venezuela, Medellin, Colombia, Montevideo, Uruguay, Paramaribo, Surinam, Quito, Ecuador, Recife, Brazil, Rio de Janeiro, Brazil, Salvador, Brazil, Santiago, Chile, Sao Paulo, Brazil

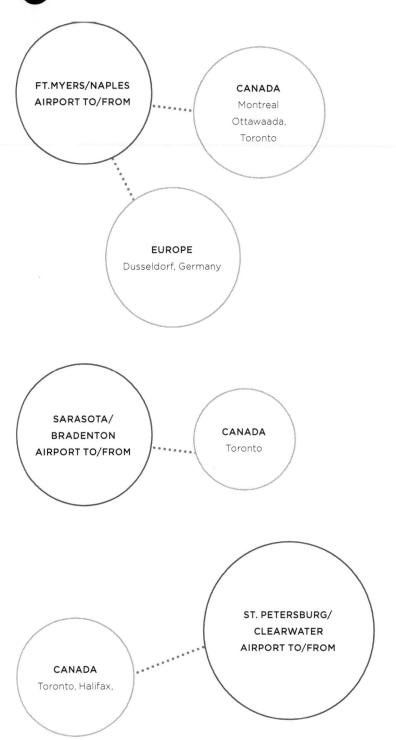

FT.MYERS/NAPLES AIRPORT TO/FROM

CANADA
Montreal
Ottawaada,
Toronto

EUROPE
Dusseldorf, Germany

SARASOTA/ BRADENTON AIRPORT TO/FROM

CANADA
Toronto

ST. PETERSBURG/ CLEARWATER AIRPORT TO/FROM

CANADA
Toronto, Halifax,

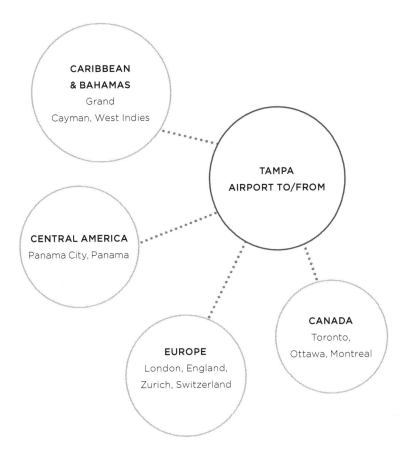

CARIBBEAN
& BAHAMAS
Grand
Cayman, West Indies

CENTRAL AMERICA
Panama City, Panama

TAMPA
AIRPORT TO/FROM

EUROPE
London, England,
Zurich, Switzerland

CANADA
Toronto,
Ottawa, Montreal

MEETING PEOPLE FROM YOUR HOME COUNTRY

As the previous section on international air travel illustrates, Florida is a state that attracts a myriad of global immigrants and visitors. In fact, a study in Florida public schools determined that there are over 200 different first languages spoken in the homes of Florida school children. People of many nationalities choose to settle here and make Florida home, so we just want to make mention of the extensive networks of foreigners throughout Florida. You might find them to be great resources as you think about where to live, get settled in, and start making connections. Also, when you are looking to watch a sporting event or celebrate a holiday that is big in your home country, you may very well find others to share your time and traditions with! There are so many formal (and less formal) groups throughout the state, so the best way to discover is to perform internet searches specific to your city/town on Facebook and the web.

4
CHAPTER

MANAGING A FLORIDA HOME WHILE ABROAD

ABSENT OWNERS

In Florida there are significant numbers of property owners, U.S. residents and foreigners alike, who use their home only seasonally, part-time or for holidays. In some communities, as many as 30- 50 percent of the residents may be part-time or seasonal. This means it is quite common for people to simply lock the door and leave for large periods of time, if not most of the year. Because of this, there are also many resources available in case you would like to hire people or companies to help care for anything—big or small —while you are away.

The choice is yours as to how much or little you want to do with respect to keeping up with the bills, maintenance, and guests/renters if applicable. It can range from managing everything yourself, to hiring a property management company to take care of everything so you don't ever have to lift a finger. If you want to rent your home when you are not there, you will also have a variety of options to help manage that whole process as we discuss in detail in the next section.

Maintaining Your Home While You're Away

We would venture to say that when they are ready to leave, a great deal of Florida property owners will simply lock the door and go. They may adjust the thermostat and turn off the hot water heater in order to conserve energy, as well as shut off the main water line into the house to ensure no water issues arise, but that is about the extent of it.

We discussed utilities in our earlier chapter on Owning a Home in Florida. As we mentioned there, all these companies are set up to send out bills electronically, so in this respect it does not matter where you are. If you would like to have someone else to take care of the bills so you don't have to bother with them at all, you can always set up a relationship with a property manager or concierge (see below) and simply turn everything over to them.

AUTHOR'S NOTE

Speaking from our family's experience, we all love to travel for extended periods so we also leave our home vacant frequently. We do this with piece of mind that our garden maintenance and pool servicing crew (the two services that work on auto-pilot in Florida) show up with unquestionable reliability. So we ourselves, like so many of our clients, can leave everything behind without a worry.

We think it is useful to point out, that one of the things many of our buyers are accustomed to worrying about when leaving their homes vacant in colder climates is freezing pipes. This is never an issue in Florida. Precisely because we do not have to contend with the challenges of snow and ice, it is pretty easy to just go!

Whether you are living in a house or condo, it is always nice to find a person, friend, or neighbor who can check in on your home occasionally just to make sure nothing looks amiss. If you are living in a condo, many of these considerations are easily handled by the office or maintenance staff. They are accustomed to looking after the units of their residents. And with the widespread use of Smartphones, it is really easy to send a picture, or even a short video, should something require your attention.

MAIL

In the U.S it is possible to have two addresses, one your mailing address—which can be a post office box where you receive your mail—and two your actual physical home address. Even if you are not set up to receive any official mail (such as utility bills, vendor bills, or tax bills) to your property's physical address, it is quite common for advertisements to arrive in the mailbox at the end of your driveway. The way some absentee owners choose to handle this is to have the local post office hold their mail, have someone pull all the mail out of your mailbox occasionally, or remove the mailbox entirely and no mail will be delivered (this is not usually an option if you live in a condominium). If you do the latter, it is important that you ensure you have opted to receive any utility bills, vendor/service provider bills, as well as your annual property tax bill electronically, or to your mailing address.

GARDEN AND POOL SERVICE

Given our wonderful sub-tropical climate, the grass and vegetation in Florida can grow quite rapidly, especially during the summer months. It is quite common—to be clearer it really is the norm—for property owners, even those that are full-time residents, to hire a landscaping service to come throughout the year to cut the grass and trim the foliage. Those who have pools hire a pool service that shows up every week to clean and maintain the pool/spa. We like to tell our clients who may not be as familiar with how things work here in Florida, that the garden and pool guys are two of the most reliable service providers you could find anywhere. They are a part of the fabric of the Florida lifestyle and they show up like clockwork, provided you have a reputable one. (Note: Ask your Realtor for recommendations!) And they are completely accustomed to working with absentee owners, sometimes they never see the homeowner, they just do their work and send the bill.

PROPERTY MANAGER

If you prefer, you may opt to hire a property manager to take care of anything in your absence. This can be an individual or a property management company. They can be responsible for things such as making sure the house remains clean, making sure all appliances and HVAC (heating, ventilation and AC) systems remain in working order, and flushing the toilets to maintain water flow. They may also make themselves available to let in any service providers that need to enter the property. It may provide you with piece of mind to have someone available and accountable who can also provide regular reports on the property.

CONCIERGE SERVICE

A concierge service is comparable to a personal assistant. They can provide some of the same services as a management company, for instance going into your home once a week to check that everything is in good order. But they can also be called on to help you in any way imaginable—almost literally. They are set up so that you tell them what you need and they get it done. Need the pantry filled before your guests arrive? Want help getting a car hired for you when you come in town? Want them to get you opera tickets to surprise your loved one with a special night on the town? You will likely be able to find either an individual or a company that will provide concierge services in your area. Some even have a special service for watching people's homes. In general, they bill by the hour.

RENTING YOUR PROPERTY

One of the fantastic opportunities when you own a home or condo in any one of Florida's many vacation/winter destinations is the ability to rent the property when you are not using it. Depending on the area in which you own and the type of property, there is a wide range of demand for rentals, including weekly, monthly, seasonal, or annual rentals. If you buy correctly, this can be a rewarding investment. A great example we like to share is one of our clients from France who purchased a beachfront condo for the family to use twice a year, once in December and once in May (for a total of five to six weeks). Their goal was to cover expenses on the property as well as the costs of their holidays. They use the onsite management and rental office, which handles all the bookings, cleaning and maintenance, as well as handling the rental sales tax that must be filed regularly. Our clients made sure to establish a good relationship with the onsite staff and prepared their condo well for rental. Now, two years later, their annual cash flow yield is four to five percent on their investment and they holiday for free.

Preparing Your Rental Property

Some key guidance we provide clients who want to rent their property is to invest some time and energy into getting the property ready for rental. (note: If your property is strictly an investment property which you will rent out full-time on an annual basis, some of the following comments regarding furnishings and how to prepare the property may not apply as you will be marketing it to a different audience.) When people rent a vacation home, they of course want the most they can get for their price range. Those properties that have the best location and conveniences, newer furnishings and updates, are clean, and come fully equipped, will naturally draw in more renters and command higher rental rates.

It's important to anticipate renters' needs and comforts, whether that be appliances and electronics, excellent kitchen equipment, or good linens and bedding. Having friends and family stay in the property for a week is a really good way of determining what's missing. **It's worth investing the time and money into these details, as you want the renters to come back year after year, and refer friends and family to your property based on their positive experience.**

In addition to having your home fully equipped, it helps that it be free of clutter, that the rooms have good flow in the way they are furnished and decorated, and the interior be prepared to be "photo ready." Attention should also be paid to the exterior so that it has good "curb appeal." For the latter, that may mean adding some color in terms of plants or flowers to the exterior. You may have a good eye for this on your own, but there are also a myriad of people you could hire from landscape designers to interior decorators or professional stagers to help you in the process.

Photography

Having great professional photography is paramount to marketing your rental. In today's world consumers "shop" online for everything, and no matter how wonderful a description you create, no one will read it if they are not first captured by the photos. **Every rental agent we meet tells us that the properties with the best photography always have higher occupancy rates as well as command a premium in rental price.** It is critical to prepare the interior and exterior so that it "shows" well in order to immediately capture the attention of prospective renters. Hiring a professional photographer is not very expensive, perhaps somewhere in the range of $100- $250 depending entirely on the size of the property being photographed. Including photography of the setting, whether that be a swimming pool, outdoor entertainment area, waterfront, beach, places that are in walking distance, etc., are all important elements to include to tell the story of your property and the experience your renters will enjoy when staying there.

Managing Your Rental

Just as you have many options to manage your property when you are away, there are a myriad of choices available to you in terms of how much or how little you want to be involved in renting your property. The type of property you own and the frequency of the rental (weekly, monthly, seasonally, annually) also plays a large part in dictating what makes the most sense for your situation.

We suggest you consider what aspects you might enjoy doing yourself and outsource the other parts. You can opt to handle the marketing yourself by using well established vacation rental websites such as, *www.Homeaway.com* or *www.AirBnB.com*, and then have a rental agent to handle everything from there. You can choose to handle all the communications with your renters, as well as the accounting, and then call in any service providers as needed. You can have one or more individuals that you trust handle any part of your choosing. Or, if you want to be totally uninvolved, you can hire a professional rental (also referred to as leasing) agent. Below we detail the extent of services and value a rental agent can provide. Some of these decisions may be dictated by the type of property you own, so let's discuss a bit more about the scenarios with condos vs. single family homes.

Condominiums

Every condominium association has a rental policy. Most of the time the policy defines the maximum number of times per year that a unit can be rented out, and/or the minimum length of time permitted (one week, one month, etc). Some condo associations go a step further, and do not allow the new owner to rent out their property until they have owned it for at least a year or more. All of these policies are in place based upon what type of experience the homeowners want for themselves at the property. For example, if you own a condo where the rental policy is a weekly minimum and you are a full-time resident, each week when you go hang out at the pool, there may be a new set of visitors.

If you own a unit in a condominium complex that is set up for short-term (usually weekly) holiday rentals, then there's usually a management team on site. As we described in the case with one of our French clients, this team takes care of every detail of advertising, booking, cleaning, maintaining the unit, accounting and filing the rental sales tax charged to the renters in exchange for 15-20 percent of the rental income. We would advise getting to know this team, as the better relationship you have with them, the better they're going to represent your interests and take care of your renters.

If you buy in a condominium complex that stipulates that you can only have longer term renters (such as several months) or restrictions on the number of rentals a year— typically they'll have a management office responsible for the care and management of the whole complex. This office will go and fix issues that arise with the building and the grounds etc. But if you plan on renting your property you may need an outside rental agent or rental management company to take care of finding and placing the tenant, resolving any issues with tenants, collecting rent and filing taxes, etc.

Single Family Homes

There are many directions you can go when renting your single family home, starting with the duration of rentals, which can span from weekly to annually. Again, if you choose to rent for shorter durations you will likely want the help of a rental agent or rental management company. Annual rentals are less work in the sense that there is not the turnover, so you may choose the do most things yourself. However, you still must have a good maintenance team in place to respond should your tenant call with issues.

Hiring a Rental (A.K.A. Leasing) Agent

A rental agent may be independent, work as part of a rental (leasing) management company, or be a Realtor. Most of the time, they are very flexible as to how much or how little you want them to handle. As a baseline, they tend to earn 15-20 percent of the rental income in exchange for their services. As with anything, finding an excellent rental agent is important. They can be pivotal advisors to you through the process of deciding how to prepare your property for rental, positioning your rental according to the target market, setting up the marketing, etc. Again, your Realtor will likely have some experience with rental agents in your market and be able to provide recommendations.

Rental agents aim to do a good job for landlords, because the more rentals they're managing the better for their business. There is a lot of competition for tenant dollars, so you want to know how your rental agent will market your property. You want to find a person or company that is responsive for tenants too, because if your renters leave feeling they were well taken care of, they will give your property good ratings, refer you to others, and likely return themselves.

You can use some of the things we list here to ask questions/interview prospective rental agents. It is a great way to learn yourself as well as get a feel for how professional and knowledgeable that agent is to determine if you would like to hire them.

Rental agents are set up handle a wide variety of tasks for their clients. Again, because they are very knowledgeable about the local rental market, they can provide invaluable information and resources, helping you to avoid common pitfalls, save money, and maximize profits. They also typically have in-house crews of service professionals or longstanding relationships with local vendors that allow them to take care of home maintenance—whether routine or emergency—quickly and efficiently.

Here are some of the ways a rental agent can add value and make your life as a landlord easier:

PRICING RENTAL PROPERTIES

- An experienced rental agent will put his or her deep knowledge of your specific local market to work in setting the rent for your property in order to maximize your cash flow while keeping vacancies low.

ADVERTISING VACANCIES AND SHOWING AVAILABLE UNITS

- Rental agents know the best places to advertise when it comes to attracting quality tenants. And they're available to conduct showings of your unit during business hours, in the evenings, and on weekends.

SCREENING TENANTS

- Rental agents often employ sophisticated scoring systems that take into account multiple factors when it comes to selecting the right tenant for your rental.

PREPARING LEASE CONTRACTS

- Rental agents are experts at crafting clear, thorough agreements that include key policies on a wide range of issues.

ONGOING PROPERTY MANAGEMENT

- Often rental agents provide ongoing, comprehensive rental management once your unit has been rented. This includes everything from collecting rent, managing relationships with tenants, and handling routine and emergency maintenance, to taking care of accounting and preparing yearly taxes.

Insurance for Your Rental Property

Even with the best tenants and preventative maintenance, unexpected things can and do happen. We feel it is important to ensure that you have an insurance policy in place that will cover the cost of damages and accidents. What type and how much insurance you choose is a business decision. All property owners must choose their own risk tolerance and the costs associated with the different options and values available.

Because insurance companies view condominiums as easily rentable assets, it tends to be easy and relatively inexpensive to build in a rental policy. Most insurance policies for condominiums make it easy to add a "rental endorsement" (insurance speak for "damage caused by renters") for about $100 per year. This coverage may specify the length of rental allowable, i.e. anywhere from nightly rentals to annual rentals.

If you have a single family house that you will use yourself and rent out periodically, we recommend you discuss your scenario with your insurance broker to understand the different options and costs associated with each. For single family homes that will be used exclusively as an investment (rental) property, the insurance policy will be set up as such at the time of purchase.

Just so our readers are aware, we like to share these two additional points:

- Tenants/renters that seek short-term vacation rentals are likely to have insurance coverage on their primary home that also covers the property that they are using when they travel

- Some landlords who have annual rentals require (in the lease agreement) that tenants/renters get a renters policy which covers any damage they may cause during their rental, including their personal belongings (i.e. clothes, technology devices, furniture), and accidents that may happen to them or others while inside the rental property.

Utilities for Rentals

For properties that rent for short periods—daily, weekly, monthly, or seasonally—the owner usually is responsible for maintaining the accounts in her/his name and paying the utilities directly. The average cost of the utilities is generally factored into the rental price. These expenses are also usually deductible from the owner's rental income, reducing the taxable income amount.

When it comes to long-term rentals, the tenant generally holds the utilities accounts in his/her own name and pays them directly. In Florida, if the payment is not made, the liability stays with the tenant who is responsible for the account. The exception to this is water/sewerage providers.

These companies may hold a landlord liable for unpaid water bills at a property. If a bill is unpaid for a certain period of time, the utility provider will typically terminate the utility at the property so that the unpaid balance does not continue to grow.

Taxes on Rental Income

FEDERAL INCOME TAX ON RENTAL INCOME

When a non-resident individual owns rental real estate in the U.S., there are two alternatives for reporting and paying U.S. income taxes. **Most non-residents choose to report the rental income on a U.S. income tax return, Form 1040NR.** They must report the rental income received; however, all expenses associated with the property are deductible against the rental income. These expenses include property taxes, insurance, mortgage interest, repairs, etc. In addition, a calculated amount for depreciation is also deducted. A personal exemption of roughly $3700 is also allowed. After taking all these deductions into account, the majority of owners do not have any taxable income.

If there is no taxable income, then there is no tax to pay. However, even if the foreign property owner has no taxable income, or is making a loss, the income tax returns still need to be filed. In the future when the property is making money, tax can be offset by bringing forward previous years' losses. In addition, any home-buying start-up expenses (filing fees, title insurance, home inspections, new paint and flooring, etc.) accumulate and carry forward indefinitely for annual taxes. If any losses that have been carried forward annually still remain when the property is sold, they become available to offset profit on sale.

AUTHOR'S NOTE

As we continue to emphasize throughout our book, it pays to consult a tax expert at the outset of your fact-finding so you are armed with good information to plan ahead. With good planning and accounting, most global buyers do not end up owing taxes from rental income.

The individual may choose to not file an income tax return in the U.S. to report the rental income. In this case, 30 percent of the **gross** rental income must be remitted to the Internal Revenue Service. If a rental agent handles the rental, the agent must withhold and remit the 30 percent as rent is collected. If no rental agent is involved, then the non-resident owner is obligated to pay the 30 percent to the Internal Revenue Service.

In order to avoid the 30 percent withholding on the gross rental income, the non-resident owner must provide a Form W 8ECI to the rental agent. The Form W 8ECI informs the rental agent that the owner is electing to treat the rental activity as a U.S trade or business and obligates the owner to file a U.S. income tax return to report the rental activity. The nonresident owner must also apply for and obtain a U.S. taxpayer identification number (ITIN) if they have not previously obtained one or if they do not possess a U.S. social security number. This identification number can be obtained by filing a Form W 7 with the Internal Revenue Service.

SHORT-TERM RENTAL SALES TAX

In Florida there are sales taxes on rentals under six months in length. This is usually charged to the renters, then collected, filed, and submitted by the property owner or manager to the local government entity. For rentals than six months no sales tax is applicable.

5

CHAPTER

SELLING
YOUR HOME

THE PROCESS

The primary two reasons people sell their home are because of a major life event, or a desired change of lifestyle. Life events include adding new family members, grown up children moving out, death of a loved one, marriage, divorce, job promotion or loss, and retirement. Many of these circumstances cause a seller to need to change locations, to upsize, downsize, simplify, or somehow craft their next stage of life via a property change.

What's also unique to certain areas of Florida is that even within a very small geographic area, there are many different lifestyle experiences available. It is not uncommon for people to live in one location for a couple years, and then yearn to try a different experience in the same city. This was a totally new concept to Lisa, who did not grow up in Florida but moved here just after we married. She was surprised to see the frequency with which so many properties turned over in Sarasota. Being that it is a resort town, you could opt to live on a golf course, then move to a beach front condo, then live right in the historic downtown area where you can walk everywhere, then move back to the water where you can have your own boat dock. Your best lifestyle match today maybe different to the experience you want in two, five, or ten years.

When you choose to sell your house, you may choose to sell it yourself or use a Realtor. In our chapter on the buying process, we discuss in detail what Realtors bring to the table as well as how to interview them and choose one that you feel good working with. All the guidance we provide in these prior sections is just as relevant when you are selling your property. You may already have a great relationship with a Realtor from your purchase, in which case you can elect to use them again.

If you would like a recommendation from our team for a Realtor that we have personally screened, you can use the **Investments in Florida Realtor Referral Program** which can be found at *www.InvestmentsInFlorida.com*. This program is a special resource for our readers, offering one of the best ways to find a Florida Realtor.

These individuals have all been personally pre-assessed by us, show the skill and experience we demand in an agent, and are experts in their region.

What Role do Realtors Play in Selling?

A Realtor works as the "point-person" to manage the entire selling process. They will advise you on how to prepare your property to market, set the pricing, handle all the marketing, communications, questions from other agents and potential buyers, manage showings, and advise you of feedback from showings. He or she will guide you on how to achieve the most favourable outcome throughout the process, especially during negotiations of the contract and with any subsequent issues that may arise during the due diligence process. **Another paramount benefit to listing with a Realtor is that your property gets listed on the MLS**. As we talk about in the buying section, by having your property in the MLS the listing is accessible to all Realtors working your area, as well as syndicated to hundreds of consumer internet sites. Since 90 percent of buyers work with a Realtor, and 92 percent of all buyers search the internet during the home buying process, this is a key advantage.

Preparing and Staging the Property for Sale

The underlying goal in preparing your property is to make it as easy as possible for other people to buy. That means making it easy for buyers to visualize the use of the space and themselves in it. Most buyers are not keen on needing to do work to a property, they just want to enjoy the home, or rent it out straight away.

Many owners grow accustomed to the eccentricities of their homes without realizing that a few simple changes or improvements could drastically increase the marketability of their property. Sometimes it's as simple as a fresh paint job, a deep clean, removing excess furniture and clutter, making minor repairs, or tearing up carpet to reveal hardwood floors. Or a Realtor might suggest larger improvements—like renovating a kitchen or bathroom—that will considerably raise the value of the home.

In many situations we recommend to our clients that they consult a professional stager before they list their home. In our opinion, staging a house is a very strategic way to improve the look and feel. We have seen firsthand dramatic transformation of interior spaces through staging. A stager has an eye for how to use fixtures, furniture, colors, and accessories in such a way that makes a home look bigger, brighter, cleaner, warmer, more loving and, best of all, more appealing to home buyers.

Listing Agreement

Here in Florida when a homeowner is selling a property, there is an exclusive contract called a Listing Agreement where the seller elects to work with one agent/broker on the sale of the house for a defined amount of time. Typically the length of a Listing Agreement is six months to one year.

As we have discussed already, many Realtors work as 'transaction agents' by default. Unless specifically stated and agreed to in writing, they don't represent either the buyer or the seller, as they are responsible for facilitating the transaction. We discuss our position on this topic at length earlier in this book and we recommend that in the listing agreement you as the seller specify you want a single agency relationship. This means the professional you hire has a fiduciary responsibility to you, they're not representing the transaction, they're representing your needs and working for you, to get the result you want. See the previous section for more on transaction agents vs. single agents.

The Importance of Price

Though we put much thought and energy into how to prepare, position, market each of our listings, we tell our clients that in the end it is all goes back to the price. It is important to establish a listing price that generates interest in the way of inquiries and showings. There are some neighbourhoods that the moment a new property comes to market everyone wants to see it because there is a high demand for the neighbourhood. However, buyers need to see value in the property and if the price is listed well above the perceived value, potential buyers may shy away from making offers.

An experienced Realtor should know all the nuances of a particular market in order to make the most accurate assessment of the maximum selling price the property can hope to achieve, without alienating buyers by over pricing. Most aim to price the property so that they can achieve a fast and smooth sale. Once the price is decided, the surest feedback will come from the market. The market will tell you quite clearly, either by lack of viewings, or lack of offers, or low offers, how accurate the listing price is.

In Florida it is quite rare that a property sells at the price it is listed. Some properties are well priced, meaning they are fairly in line with the market value, and some are not. It is incumbent on your Realtor to help any potential buyers (usually by working with their Realtor) understand the value in your property, and to try to negotiate as close to the listing price as the market data supports.

HOW TO DETERMINE PRICE

The value of every property as established by the property appraiser for tax purposes is public record, meaning it's available for anyone to know. You can access this information on the municipal website. This is one data point that people reference, although this is typically lower than the true market value. A competitive market analysis (CMA) using similar properties in a neighborhood that have sold in the recent past is the most relevant estimate of what a buyer should be willing to pay for your property. In situations where you own a very unique type of luxury property against which it is difficult to find comparable sales data, it may be helpful to hire an independent appraiser. (See our discussion on appraisers in previous section Professionals you Need and What They Do.)

SELLER'S DISCLOSURE

In Florida it is the homeowner's responsibility to disclose any issues or material defects about properties which are not readily visible or known to the buyer. This is referred to as the Seller's Disclosure. There is not a particular form that is required to convey this information though if you are working with a Realtor they will likely have a format they like to work with. The Florida Association of Realtors has a standard Seller's Disclosure form available. We provide a sample of this document for you in our appendix.

PRE-SALE INSPECTION

There are certain situations when we recommend that the seller conduct a home inspection before listing the property. This is most appropriate when the property owner spends limited, or no time in the property. The advantage of inspecting a home before putting it on the market is to avoid being surprised by unseen defects in the property. Most buyers will request an inspection after making an offer, and hidden problems like cracked foundations and rusty plumbing could break the deal. It's better to fix those problems before trying to sell the house, and this also optimizes your chance to command a higher price for your property.

AUTHOR'S NOTE

If we are dealing with a property that is very outdated and/or in disrepair there may be a chance that the next buyer tears it down and builds a new home. It still may make sense to perform certain improvements/repairs in order to achieve the highest market price. We explain to our clients that the buyer will place zero value on the structure if they see it as unsalvageable, and will only want to pay land value. However, if the house has redeemable value, the tear-down buyer will still have to pay something for the structure even though they will not use it.

There are two ways to sell a house: 'as is' or 'with warranty'. The former is effectively saying up front "buyer beware and do your homework". This is typically used by sellers who don't spend a lot of time at the property, or for older homes if you prefer to avoid being obliged to make any repairs. If you opt for the 'as is' route, you may still choose to make repairs or agree to offset the costs to do so, depending on what comes up in the home inspection report. One thing we know is if an issue is big enough to be of concern to any buyer, it is something you will be motivated to fix anyway.

With the 'with warranty' option, you are responsible for all major systems being in working condition. If you are living in the home, on top of all the maintenance, and you are not worried about any issues this may be the route to go, as you could potentially generate a higher selling price than selling 'as-is'.

Marketing Your Property

Just as we go into detail in the Photography section of the previous chapter, the marketing of your property starts with excellent **professional** photographs. Everyone, whether other Realtors via the MLS, or consumers via the myriad of real estate internet sites, will determine their interest level by first looking at the pictures.

When you're selling a home in Florida it's important to remember the property is being marketed to two constituents:

CONSUMERS

There are dozens and dozens of internet sites serving consumers. In our experience working with clients as well as from our own listings, we find that Realtor.com, Zillow and Trulia are the lead consumer sites. They consistently rank in the top three in web searches for any area.

REALTORS

Well over 90 percent of properties are sold by Realtors. Although many think that marketing should be consumer focused, we make the point that while this is important, the primary focus should be how to reach the Realtor community. Also remember when it comes to marketing your property, only Realtors can post to the MLS, which is where other Realtors go to source property for their active buyers.

Choosing to Sell Your Home Yourself

Some homeowners opt to sell their homes themselves as they would like to save the commission rate. One point we would like to make here is that most people searching for a home are working with a Realtor, so it is not uncommon for those homes being marketed as "For Sale by Owner" to state that Realtors are welcome, inferring that should a Realtor bring them a buyer, the seller will offer them a commission. Otherwise, a Realtor may not have an incentive to show properties which are not listed in the MLS where commissions are clearly defined.

There are many resources available offering guidance on how to sell your home yourself. There are also websites such as ***www.forsalebyowner.com*** to list your property. Just be aware that you still must be informed about the state and federal guidelines as you still need to comply.

TAX IMPLICATIONS

Capital Gains

Capital gains tax is effectively tax you pay on the profit you've made on your property's appreciation since you bought it. The capital gains tax is calculated on the profit made from the sale of real estate. The profit is revenue (sale price less purchase price) minus expenses. An accountant will guide you what qualifies as expenses. We advise that you keep very accurate records with the costs associated with the purchase and sale of your property and everything in between. This may include things that are not as obvious such as travel expenses to visit your property. The capital gains tax rate applied to your profit will depend on how you hold title, and the amount of profit that you will generate.

Foreign Investment Real Property Tax Act (FIRPTA)

In the United States, the driving force behind FIRPTA is to ensure foreign investors fulfill their tax obligations to the Internal Revenue Service (IRS). **One of the provisions FIRPTA makes to accomplish this is to make the BUYER of a property from a global SELLER liable for any unpaid capital gains taxes that the seller may owe because of a profit realized from the sale.** (Yes, you may need to read that a second time, it is not a typo.) Rest assured, when we first heard about this ourselves, we found it not exactly intuitive. We suggest that with the help of an accounting professional it does not need to be a cumbersome process to work through. Professionals that do this line of work everyday see the requirements/responsibilities as very straightforward. And as a reminder, the fees for this work tend to be small since for the professionals facilitating the process they are routine.

The standard course of action is for the buyer to withhold ten percent of the money that the seller is supposed to receive, and send it to the IRS within 20 days of the buyer closing on the purchase. The IRS has a list of exceptions that relieve the buyer of this responsibility.

Two of the basic exceptions that release the buyer from withholding the full ten percent are:

1. A Withholding Certificate that excuses withholding. The IRS is required to respond to withholding certification requests within 90 days of receipt. They are submitted by the seller to the IRS

2. If the transaction price of the property is $300,000 or less, and the buyer and/or their family intend to use it as a residence or for personal purposes at least 50 percent of the time, for two years following the purchase

Source: *www.irs.gov/Individuals/International-Taxpayers/ Exceptions-from-FIRPTA-Withholding*

If you are reading this from the perspective of a global seller, we encourage you (and your advisors) to make sure that you give the buyer clear information as it relates to FIRPTA. If your objective is to not have the ten percent withheld, you must give them adequate time to do their due diligence and leave them comfortable that the IRS will not pursue them (the buyer) for uncollected/unpaid obligations that are owed to the IRS by you (the seller).

Applying for Withholding Certificate Prior to Sale

It generally takes 90 days for the IRS to issue the certificate, which states the amount to be withheld as zero. So if this is the route you're going, make sure you allow enough time for the certificate to be issued, otherwise the ten percent will still be due 20 days after closing.

If the time lag creates a problem and closing has to be conducted before the certificate is issued, then the ten percent can be deducted from the sale, and held in escrow by the closing agent until the certificate is issued.

Tax Returns and Refunds

Regardless of whether the ten percent was withheld or not and whether you owe money or not, the IRS requires you to file a tax return. If you are due a refund, be aware that the IRS begins processing tax returns and refunds at the beginning of the next calendar year.

1031 Exchange

A 1031 Exchange is a mechanism for real estate investors to delay (or defer) taxes on the gain they realized from the sale of their real estate investment. This mechanism is available to all owners/sellers of real estate in the U.S. Global sellers have a few additional steps to take because of the FIRPTA rule. As we wrote earlier, in order to ensure that a seller does not skip out on their obligation to pay their U.S. tax the IRS established FIRPTA in the 1980s.

FOR ALL SELLERS WHO WANT TO DEFER THE GAIN, THEY ARE REQUIRED TO:

1. Place the proceeds of the sale into an escrow account of a qualified intermediary

2. Identify up to three properties targeted for investment within 45 calendar days of the sale of the prior investment

3. The investor must close on the purchase of one of those three properties within 180 calendar days of the sale of the prior investment.

Generically, these are the basic steps for all investors. There is also a fee for the 1031 Exchange. The global investor will also have to comply with the FIRPTA requirements in addition to the general investor requirements.

In our experience, 1031 exchanges are straightforward to facilitate. There are a few rules that must be followed explicitly, and a few boxes which must be ticked.

When you are contemplating the sale of your investment property, work with your accountant and Realtor to figure out if in your situation it makes sense to do a 1031 exchange, or if it would be better to simply pay the taxes on the profit. Once you calculate each financial scenario and take into account your personal objectives, it usually will be pretty clear which is the better option for your personal situation.

FINAL POINTS ON CAPITAL GAINS TAX ADVANTAGES FOR RESIDENTS

In the U.S., a married couple is able to earn $500,000 on the sale of their **primary** residence tax-free. If you are single this number is $250,000. One way to realize a non-taxable gain is by making your U.S. home your primary residence. Obviously if this is the case you must have an applicable residency visa. If you are a resident in your house for 183 days per year, or two years out of a five-year period, and have owned the property for at least two years, then each resident owner is entitled to $250,000 in tax-free earnings. As a working example: if you purchased a home for $500,000 as a couple, and two years later sell it for $1 million, then the $500,000 gain can be split between two resident spouses as income, and there will be no tax on that gain.

KNOWING YOUR RESIDENCY STATUS FOR TAX PURPOSES—THE 183 DAY RULE

You can be taxed for U.S. income tax purposes either as a resident or as a non-resident. Residents are required to report their worldwide income to the U.S. taxing authorities. Non-residents are required to report only income arising from U.S. sources. There are several ways you can be treated as a resident for U.S. income tax purposes. U.S. citizens are always U.S. income tax residents, regardless of where they live. Under most circumstances, an individual who obtains a Green Card (which allows the holder to reside permanently in the U.S.) will be taxed as a resident.

Even if you are not a U.S. citizen, you could be determined to be an income tax resident in the U.S. merely by the number of days in which you are physically present in the U.S. during the current calendar year, or a combination of days over the last three years. If you're physically present in the U.S. for 183 days or more in a calendar year, you are treated as a U.S. income tax resident.

AFTERWORD

As we conclude our voyage leading you through the process of buying Florida property, we want to leave you with three main points. Firstly that Florida real estate is a safe, secure and savvy investment. Secondly, that it's straightforward to buy, sell and enjoy your property here. And thirdly, that you won't regret for a second the lifestyle upgrades which owning a Florida home can bring you. But if there is one thing that we hope you take away from this book, it's that *the opportunity to live and play in Florida is a very real possibility and within reach of many people.*

We hope you are now equipped with the knowledge and tools you need to start your journey with confidence. For us, we live the Florida lifestyle every day and truly enjoy witnessing our clients' joy as they settle into what they seek here. Please don't hesitate to contact us to learn more about the opportunities throughout the state and how we can help you achieve your dream.

Abundant Sunshine, Lisa & Lee

- To access the complimentary **Investments in Florida Realtor Referral Program** for our readers, visit *www.InvestmentsInFlorida.com*

- You may visit *www.InvestmentsInFlorida.com* to start seeing Florida properties, or to sign up for our free reader newsletter offering valuable content, advice, and current market updates

- If you would like to share your story about buying/investing in Florida real estate we would love to hear from you. We may even include it in our next edition! You may submit it to: *sunshine@InvestmentsInFlorida.com*

- If you have any feedback about content in the book, or suggestions on additional material you think would be helpful to other global buyers write us at *feedback@InvestmentsInFlorida.com*

- If you enjoyed our book we would be immeasurably grateful for your review on Amazon.

Our Ethos

Together Lee and Lisa founded their philanthropic organisation Global Social Housing. Through this non-profit, in a ground-breaking partnership with the Peace Corps, they aim to address part of the vast global need for housing by building self-progressing communities. The UN has identified slum housing as the defining issue of this century and by breaking the poverty cycle at its critical point this program transforms lives and communities.

Please visit ***www.globalsocialhousing.org*** to learn how you can be involved in the journey.

6

CHAPTER

APPENDICES

SUMMARY

In our appendices we endeavor to provide supplemental information that may assist you in choosing the location to invest in a Florida home and lifestyle, along with a glossary of real estate terms for your reference. We also provide you with sample excerpts of the most common documents you will likely encounter in the process. While these are only partial examples, they are intended to provide you with some familiarity of the types of forms you may come across in a Florida real estate transaction.

1. Population of Florida Cities

2012 POPULATIONS ESTIMATES* FOR

20 LARGEST METROPOLITAN AREAS IN FLORIDA

1	Miami-Fort Lauderdale-West Palm Beach, FL	5,762,717
2	Tampa-St.Petersburg-Clearwater, FL	2,842,878
3	Orlando-Kissimmee-Sanford	2,223,674
4	Jacksonville, FL	1,377,850
5	North Port-Sarasota-Bradenton, FL	720,042
6	Cape Coral-Ft Myers, FL	645,293
7	Lakeland-Winter Haven, FL	616,158
8	Deltona-Daytona Beach-Ormond Beach	595,309
9	Palm Bay-Melbourne-Titusville, FL	547,307
10	Pensacola-Ferry Pass-Brent, FL	461,227
11	Port St. Lucie, FL	432,683
12	Tallahassee, FL	375,371
13	Ocala, FL	335,125
14	Naples-Immokalee-Marco Island, FL	332,427
15	Gainesville, FL	268,232
16	Crestview-Fort Walton Beach-Destin, FL	247,665
17	Panama City, FL	187,621
18	Punta Gorda, FL	162,449
19	Sebastian-Vero Beach, FL	140,567
20	Homosassa Springs, FL	139,360

* As estimated by United States Census Bureau

2. International Airports

1. Miami International Airport

2. Orlando International Airport

3. Fort Lauderdale-Hollywood International Airport

4. Tampa International Airport

5. Southwest Florida International Airport

6. Palm Beach International Airport

7. Jacksonville International Airport

8. Pensacola International Airport

9. Sarasota Bradenton International Airport

10. Orlando Sanford International Airport

11. St. Petersburg-Clearwater International Airport

12. Northwest Florida Beaches International Airport

13. Key West International Airport

14. Daytona Beach International Airport

15. Melbourne International Airport

3. Frequently Used Florida Real Estate Terms

Amortization

The process by which mortgages are paid off—with a proportion of each payment being distributed toward the principle and the interest. To begin with, a larger percentage is paid towards the interest than the principle. Borrowers may pay more often or increase the value of their payments in order to reduce the amount of interest they pay over the term of the mortgage.

Appraisal

An assessment of the value of a property for tax purposes.

Appraiser

A professional certified and licensed in the state of Florida by the Department of Professional and Business Regulation.

Approved Lender

A lending institution such as a bank that is authorized by the Government to make loans to consumers.

Closing Costs

The costs you pay in addition to the price of a property on the day you officially transfer ownership of the home from the previous owner. Including: legal fees, disbursements, and transfer fees. They usually range from 1.5 percent to 3 percent of the purchase price of the home.

Closing Date	The date when the sale of the property becomes final and the new owner takes ownership of the home. The day of closing belongs to the buyer. All expenses (utilities, taxes, etc.) are the responsibility of the buyer beginning on closing day.
Conventional Mortgage	A mortgage for up to 80% of the property's value. Insurance is usually not needed for this type of mortgage.
Co-pay	Usually in health insurance, when the insured pays a specified amount of the expenses for services such as doctor's visits, prescriptions etc.
Counteroffer	If your original offer to the seller is not accepted, the seller may counteroffer. A counteroffer usually changes something from your original offer, such as the price or closing date.
Credit Report	The report detailing your credit history, that the lender uses to decide your creditworthiness for a mortgage.
Curb Appeal	How appealing a house looks from the street. A property with good curb appeal will have a well maintained exterior and attractive landscaping.

Deed	The legal document signed by the seller, two witnesses, and the notarized to transfer property ownership.
Default	Failing to abide by the terms of a mortgage agreement and make timely payments. If you default on (fail to make) payments, your lender may start legal action to take possession of your home.
Delinquency	Failure to make mortgage payments on time.
Deposit	Money placed in an escrow account by a buyer when they make an offer to buy a property. The deposit is typically held by the buyer's lawyer, real estate broker, or closing agent until the sale is completed
Down Payment	The portion of the price of a property that is not financed by the mortgage, which must be paid out of your own savings, finances or other sources. This money plus the mortgage amount will add up to the purchase price of the home.
Foreclosure	The process of a lender taking possession of your home if you fail to keep up payments (default) on a mortgage. The lender sells the home to recover the mortgage debts you have failed to pay.

High-Ratio Mortgage	A mortgage for more than 80 percent of the property's value. These types of mortgages usually require mortgage loan insurance.
Home inspector	A home inspector is licensed and regulated by the Department of Business and Professional Regulation to examine a home to determine if anything is broken, needs to be replaced or is unsafe. They may also be able to determine if there have been any problems in the past.
Homeowners Insurance	This is Insurance which protects you in the case that your home or building is destroyed or damaged by fire or other hazards which are covered by the policy.
Insurance Broker	An insurance broker helps you choose and buy insurance policies such as flood insurance, homeowner's insurance, and renter's insurance. Typically they can choose from multiple options to find the right match for your needs.
Interest	The cost of borrowing money. A percentage of Interest is usually paid to the lender regularly along with repayment of the principal borrowed amount.

Municipality	A city, town or district which exists as a corporate structure, and usually its own government.
Surveyor	In Florida are professionals regulated by the Board of Professional Surveyors and Mappers. They create a map of the property to locate corners, boundaries, and distances from buildings to the property's edge so that easements and setbacks can be determined to be compliant with the municipality and neighborhood building codes. Lenders will require a survey consistent with the property's current layout.
Lawyer	Licensed by the Supreme Court to practice law in the state of Florida. Lawyers may be consulted to represent you and your interests, and review documents as a seller or buyer of property in Florida.
Lender/mortgage broker	Lenders loan you money (mortgages) to help you finance buying a home. Lenders can include banks, credit unions, trust companies, pension funds, finance companies, and insurance companies. A mortgage broker works with a variety of different lenders to get you a mortgage that meets all your needs.

| Lump Sum Prepayment | This is an extra payment which reduces the principal remaining on your mortgage, sometimes with a penalty for early repayment, sometimes without. Lump sum payments may help you pay off your mortgage more quickly, thus saving on interest costs. |

| Maturity Date | The last day of the term of the mortgage. By this date the mortgage loan must either be renewed or the balance paid in full. |

| MLS (Multiple Listing Service) | A private database which lists properties for rent and sale. The MLS allows Realtors to share information on all properties for sale in a given area so they may cooperate in the sale and purchase of listed properties. It also provides a formal structure with regards to commission sharing between parties. The MLS database is syndicated out to many companies, and is then accessed by the public easily through websites. |

| Mortgage | An agreement between a borrower and lender to loan a specified amount of money for a specified period of time for a specified price (interest) using a piece of property as a guarantee or collateral for the loan. |

Mortgage Life Insurance   Insurance which pays of your mortgage if you die, protecting your family.

Mortgage Insurance   Insurance that protects your lender in the event of you defaulting. If your mortgage is for more than 80 percent of the property's value, your lender will probably require mortgage loan insurance.

Mortgage Payment   A regular payment which often includes both principal and interest payments. It is also usually combined with a monthly payment of property taxes and homeowners' insurance.

Net Worth   Your financial worth, which is calculated by subtracting your total liabilities (everything you owe) from your total assets (everything you own).

New Home Warranty   Guarantees that any defects in a new home will be repaired.

Offer   A written offer that sets out the terms under which a buyer agrees to buy a home. Once an offer is accepted by a seller, it becomes a legally binding contract.

Operating Costs	These are the monthly expenses it costs you to run a home. Including homeowners' insurance, property taxes, maintenance, repairs and utilities.
Principal	The amount that you borrow in a loan agreement.
Property Taxes	Taxes charged by the municipality based on the municipality's property appraiser's assessed value of the property.
Realtor	A Realtor is a licensed real estate agent who is signed up to a strict standard of practice and ethics and who is a member of his or her local, state and national Realtor associations. Membership of the associations of Realtors provides educational opportunities, resources, and access to MLS databases to assist buyers and sellers in their local real estate markets.
Term	The length of time that a mortgage's is valid for under the agreed conditions, such as the interest rate agreed.

4. Residential Contract for Purchase and Sale

The following is a sample of the Florida Association of Realtors (FAR) Contract for Sale and Purchase. These forms are set up by FAR to set out the responsibilities of buyers, sellers and Realtors, and are only available to Realtors. We share this extract as a courtesy to inform our readers, should you wish to look at the form in its entirety, you can contact a Florida Realtor.

Contract for Residential Sale and Purchase   **FloridaRealtors**

1°   **1. Sale and Purchase:** _____ ("Seller")
2°   and _____ ("Buyer")
3   (the "parties") agree to sell and buy on the terms and conditions specified below the property described as:
4°   Street Address: _____
5°   City: _____ Zip Code: _____ County: _____
6°   Legal Description: _____
7°   _____ Tax ID No.: _____
8   together with all existing improvements and attached items, including fixtures; built-in furnishings; major appliances (including
9°   but not limited to range(s), refrigerator(s), dishwasher(s), washer(s), and dryer(s)); _____ (#) ceiling fans (all ceiling fans if left
10   blank); light fixtures; attached wall-to-wall carpeting; and rods, draperies, and other window treatments as of date of Buyer's
11°   initial offer. The only other items included in the purchase are: _____
12°   _____
13°   _____
14°   The following attached items are excluded from the purchase: _____
15°   _____
16   The real and personal property described above as included in the purchase is referred to as the "Property." Personal
17   property listed in this Contract is included in the purchase price, has no contributory value, and is being left for
18   Seller's convenience.
19°   **2. Purchase Price:** $_____ payable by Buyer in U.S. currency as follows:
20   All deposits will be made payable to "Escrow Agent" named below and held in escrow by:
21°   Escrow Agent's Name: _____
22°   Escrow Agent's Address: _____
23°   Escrow Agent's Phone: _____
24°   **(a)** $_____ "Initial Deposit" ($0 if left blank) **(Check if applicable)**
25°   ☐ accompanies offer
26°   ☐ to be delivered to Escrow Agent within _____ days (3 days if left blank) after
27   Effective Date
28°   **(b)** $_____ Additional deposit to be delivered to Escrow Agent by _____ or
29°   within _____ days (10 days if left blank) after Effective Date
30°   **(c)** _____ Total Financing (see Paragraph 3 below) (express as a dollar amount or percentage)
31°   **(d)** $_____ Other: _____
32°   **(e)** $_____ Balance to close (not including Buyer's closing costs, prepaid items, and prorations).
33   All funds paid at Closing must be paid by wire transfer or other Collected funds.
34   **3. Financing: (Check as applicable)**
35°   **(a)** ☐ **Buyer** will pay cash or obtain financing for the purchase of the Property. This Contract is not contingent on
36   financing or appraised value unless otherwise stated herein.
37°   **(b)** ☐ **Buyer** will apply for new ☐conventional ☐FHA ☐VA ☐other (specify) _____
38   financing specified in Paragraph 2(c) at the prevailing interest rate and loan costs based on Buyer's
39°   creditworthiness (the "Financing") within _____ days (5 days if left blank) after Effective Date and provide
40   Seller with either a written Financing commitment or approval letter ("Commitment") or written notice that
41°   Buyer is unable to obtain a Commitment within _____ days (the earlier of 30 days after Effective Date or 5
42   days before Closing Date if left blank) after Effective Date ("Commitment Period"). Buyer will keep Seller and
43   Broker fully informed about loan application status, progress, and Commitment issues and authorizes the
44   mortgage broker and lender to disclose all such information to Seller and Broker. If, after using diligence and
45   good faith, Buyer is unable to obtain a Commitment and provides Seller with written notice before expiration
46   of the Commitment Period that Buyer is unable to obtain a Commitment, either party may thereafter cancel
47   this Contract, and Buyer's deposit(s) will be refunded. Buyer's failure to timely provide Seller with written
48   notice that Buyer is unable to obtain a Commitment will result in forfeiture of Buyer's deposit(s) if Buyer fails

Buyer (_____) (_____) and Seller (_____) (_____) acknowledge receipt of a copy of this page, which is Page 1 of 9.
CRSP-13 Rev 3/13   ©2013 Florida Association of REALTORS®
Serial: formsimplicity

49 to close. Once **Buyer** provides the Commitment to **Seller**, the financing contingency is waived and **Seller** will
50 be entitled to retain the deposit(s) if the transaction does not close by the Closing Date unless (i) the Property
51 appraises below the purchase price and either the parties cannot agree on a new purchase price **or Buyer**
52 elects not to proceed, or (ii) the property related conditions of the Commitment have not been met (except
53 when such conditions are waived by other provisions of this Contract), or (iii) the loan is not funded due to
54 financial failure of **Buyer's** lender, or (iv) another provision of this Contract provides for cancellation.

55 **4. Closing Date; Occupancy:** Unless the Closing Date is specifically extended by **Seller** and **Buyer** or by any other
56 provision in this Contract, the Closing Date will prevail over all other time periods including, but not limited to,
57* financing and inspection periods. Closing of this Contract (the "Closing") will occur on _____
58 ("Closing Date") at the time established by the Closing Agent, by which time **Seller** will (i) have removed all
59 personal items and trash from the Property and swept the Property clean and (ii) deliver the deed, occupancy,
60 and possession, along with all keys, garage door openers, and access codes to **Buyer**. If on Closing Date
61 insurance underwriting is suspended, **Buyer** may postpone Closing for up to 5 days after the insurance
62 suspension is lifted. If on Closing Date funding from **Buyer's** lender(s) is not available due to Truth In Lending Act
63 (TILA) notice requirements, **Buyer** may postpone Closing for up to 5 days if necessary to satisfy TILA notice
64 requirements. If this transaction does not close for any reason, **Buyer** will immediately return all **Seller** provided
65 title evidence, surveys, association documents, and other items, failing which **Buyer** authorizes Closing Agent to
66* reimburse **Seller** $_____ ($100 if left blank) from the deposit(s) for the cost of the documents.

67 **5. Closing Procedure; Costs:** Closing will take place in the county where the Property is located and may be
68 conducted by mail or electronic means. If title insurance insures **Buyer** for title defects arising between the title
69 binder effective date and recording of **Buyer's** deed, Closing Agent will disburse at Closing the net sale proceeds
70 to **Seller** and brokerage fees to Broker as per Paragraph 19. In addition to other expenses provided in this
71 Contract, **Seller** and **Buyer** will pay the costs indicated below.
72 **(a) Seller Costs:**
73 Taxes and surtaxes on the deed
74 Recording fees for documents needed to cure title
75* Repairs and Permits: **Seller** will pay up to $_____ or _____% (1.5% if left blank) of the purchase
76* price for repairs to warranted items ("Repair Limit"); and up to $_____ or _____% (1.5% if left
77 blank) of the purchase price for wood-destroying organism treatment and repairs ("WDO Repair Limit"); and
78* up to $_____ or _____% (1.5% if left blank) of the purchase price for costs associated with closing
79 out open permits and obtaining required permits for unpermitted existing improvements ("Permit Limit").
80* Other: _____
81 **(b) Buyer Costs:**
82 Taxes and recording fees on notes and mortgages
83 Recording fees on the deed and financing statements
84 Loan expenses
85 Lender's title policy
86 Inspections
87 Survey
88 Flood insurance, homeowner's insurance, hazard insurance
89* Other: _____
90 **(c) Title Evidence and Insurance:** If **Seller** has an owner's title policy covering the Property, **Seller** will provide
91 a copy to **Buyer** and title agent within 5 days after Effective Date.
92 Check (1) or (2)
93* (1) ☐ The title evidence will be a Paragraph 10(a)(1) owner's title insurance commitment. ☐**Seller** will select
94 the title agent and Closing Agent and will pay for the owner's title policy; title search, including tax and lien
95* search; and all other fees charged by title agent and Closing Agent or ☐ **Buyer** will select the title agent
96 and Closing Agent and pay for the owner's title policy; title search, including tax and lien search; and all
97* other fees charged by title agent and Closing Agent or ☐ **Buyer** will select the title agent and Closing
98 Agent, and **Seller** will pay for the owner's title policy; title search, including tax and lien search; and all
99 other fees charged by title agent and Closing Agent.
100* (2) ☐ **Seller** will provide an abstract as specified in Paragraph 10(a)(2) as title evidence. ☐ **Seller** ☐ **Buyer**
101 will pay for the owner's title policy and select the title agent and Closing Agent. **Seller** will pay fees for title
102 searches, including tax and lien searches, before Closing, and **Buyer** will pay fees for title searches,
103 including tax and lien searches, after Closing (if any) and all other fees charged by title agent and Closing
104 Agent.
105 **(d) Prorations:** The following items will be made current (if applicable) and prorated as of the day before Closing:
106 real estate taxes (including special benefit tax assessments imposed by a community development district

5. Seller's Disclosure

The following is a sample of the Florida Association of Realtors (FAR) Seller's Disclosure form. These forms are set up by FAR to set out the responsibilities of buyers, sellers and Realtors, and are only available to Realtors. We share this extract as a courtesy to inform our readers, should you wish to look at the form in its entirety, you can contact a Florida Realtor.

Seller's Property Disclosure – Residential   FloridaRealtors®

Notice to Licensee: The **Seller** should fill out this form.

Notice to Seller: Florida law[1] requires a seller of a home to disclose to the buyer all known facts that materially affect the value of the property being sold and that are not readily observable or known by the buyer. This disclosure form is designed to help you comply with the law. However, this disclosure form may not address every significant issue that is unique to the Property. You should think about what you would want to know if you were buying the Property today; and if you need more space for additional information, comments, or explanations, check the Paragraph 10 checkbox and attach an addendum.

Notice to Buyer: The following representations are made by **Seller** and **not** by any real estate licensee. This disclosure is not a guaranty or warranty of any kind. It is not a substitute for any inspections, warranties, or professional advice you may wish to obtain. It is not a substitute for your own personal judgment and common sense. The following information is based only upon **Seller's** actual knowledge of the Property's condition. Sellers can disclose only what they actually know. **Seller** may not know about all material or significant items. You should have an independent, professional home inspection to verify the condition of the Property and determine the cost of repairs, if any. This disclosure is not a contract and is not intended to be a part of any contract for sale and purchase.

Seller makes the following disclosure regarding the property described as: _____
_____ (the "Property")

The Property is ☐owner occupied ☐tenant occupied ☐unoccupied (If unoccupied, how long has it been since **Seller** occupied the Property? _____

	Yes	No	Don't Know
1. Structures; Systems; Appliances:			
(a) Are the structures, including roofs; ceilings; walls; doors; windows; foundation; and pool, hot tub, and spa, if any, structurally sound and free of leaks?	☐	☐	☐
(b) Is seawall, if any, and dockage, if any, structurally sound?	☐	☐	☐
(c) Are existing major appliances and heating, cooling, mechanical, electrical, security, and sprinkler systems, in working condition, i.e., operating in the manner in which the item was designed to operate?	☐	☐	☐
(d) Are any of the appliances leased? If yes, which ones: _____	☐	☐	☐
(e) If any answer to questions 1(a) – 1(c) is no, please explain: _____			
2. Termites; Other Wood-Destroying Organisms; Pests:			
(a) Are termites; other wood-destroying organisms, including fungi; or pests present on the Property or has the Property had any structural damage by them?	☐	☐	☐
(b) Has the Property been treated for termites; other wood-destroying organisms, including fungi; or pests?	☐	☐	☐
(c) If any answer to questions 2(a) - 2(b) is yes, please explain: _____			
3. Water Intrusion; Drainage; Flooding:			
(a) Has past or present water intrusion affected the Property?	☐	☐	☐
(b) Have past or present drainage or flooding problems affected the Property?	☐	☐	☐
(c) Is any of the Property located in a special flood hazard area?	☐	☐	☐
(d) Is any of the Property located seaward of the coastal construction control line?	☐	☐	☐
(e) Does your lender require flood insurance?	☐	☐	☐
(f) Do you have an elevation certificate? If yes, please attach a copy.	☐	☐	☐
(g) If any answer to questions 3(a) - 3(d) is yes, please explain: _____			

---

[1] *Johnson v. Davis*, 480 So.2d 625 (Fla. 1985).

	Yes	No	Don't Know

4. Plumbing:
   (a) What is your drinking water source? ☐public ☐private ☐well ☐other

	Yes	No	Don't Know
(b) Have you ever had a problem with the quality, supply, or flow of potable water?	☐	☐	☐
(c) Do you have a water treatment system?	☐	☐	☐

      If yes, is it ☐owned ☐leased?
   (d) Do you have a ☐sewer or ☐septic system? If septic system, describe the location of each system: _____

	Yes	No	Don't Know
(e) Are any septic tanks, drain fields, or wells that are not currently being used located on the Property?	☐	☐	☐
(f) Have there been any plumbing leaks since you have owned the Property?	☐	☐	☐
(g) Are any polybutylene pipes on the Property?	☐	☐	☐

   (h) If any answer to questions 4(b), 4(c), and 4(e) - 4(g) is yes, please explain: _____
_____

5. Pools; Hot Tubs; Spas:
   Note: Florida law requires swimming pools, hot tubs, and spas that received a certificate of completion on or after October 1, 2000, to have at least one safety feature as specified by Section 515.27, Florida Statutes.
   (a) If the Property has a swimming pool, hot tub, or spa that received a certificate of completion on or after October 1, 2000, indicate the existing safety feature(s): ☐enclosure that meets the pool barrier requirements ☐approved safety pool cover ☐required door and window exit alarms ☐required door locks ☐none

	Yes	No	Don't Know
(b) Has an in-ground pool on the Property been demolished and/or filled?	☐	☐	☐

6. Sinkholes:
   Note: When an insurance claim for sinkhole damage has been made by the seller and paid by the insurer, Section 627.7073(2)(c), Florida Statutes, requires the seller to disclose to the buyer that a claim was paid and whether or not the full amount paid was used to repair the sinkhole damage.

	Yes	No	Don't Know
(a) Does past or present settling, soil movement, or sinkhole(s) affect the Property or adjacent properties?	☐	☐	☐
(b) Has any insurance claim for sinkhole damage been made?	☐	☐	☐
(c) If any insurance claim for sinkhole damage was made, was the claim paid?	☐	☐	☐
(d) If any insurance claim for sinkhole damage was paid, were all the proceeds used to repair the damage?	☐	☐	☐

   (e) If any answer to questions 6(a) - 6(c) is yes or the answer to question 6(d) is no, please explain: _____

7. Deed/Homeowners' Association Restrictions; Boundaries; Access Roads:

	Yes	No	Don't Know
(a) Are there any deed or homeowners' restrictions?	☐	☐	☐
(b) Are there any proposed changes to any of the restrictions?	☐	☐	☐
(c) Are there any resale or leasing restrictions?	☐	☐	☐
(d) Is membership mandatory in a homeowners' association?	☐	☐	☐
(e) Are fees charged by the homeowners' association?	☐	☐	☐
(f) Are any driveways, walls, fences, or other features shared with adjoining landowners?	☐	☐	☐
(g) Are there any encroachments on the Property or any encroachments by the Property's improvements on other lands?	☐	☐	☐
(h) Are there boundary line disputes or easements affecting the Property?	☐	☐	☐

   (i) Are access roads ☐private ☐public? If private, describe the terms and conditions of the maintenance agreement: _____
_____

   (j) If any answer to questions 7(a) - 7(h) is yes, please explain: _____
_____

6. Home Inspection Report

Alert Inspection Service, Inc.

Page   of

Name: Inspection #

Inspection Address:

House ☐   Villa ☐   Condo ☐   Other ☐_____   Approximate Age of the structure:_____

Occupied: Yes ☐ No ☐   Furnished: Yes ☐ No ☐

Weather: Clear ☐   Rain ☐   Other ☐ _____   Temperature:_____

Present at the time of inspection: Buyer   Seller   Realtor   Other

☐ **Inspection of occupied and furnished interiors and garages is limited due to the furniture placement, full closets and stored material in garages and/or other buildings or rooms.**

WATER SUPPLY ON:
  All bath and water supply off after inspection: Yes No All water supply to appliances set as before inspection: Yes No
  Comments:_____

AIR CONDITIONING:
  Temperature setting before inspection: Yes No   Set temperature after inspection: Yes No
  Comments:_____

APPLIANCES: Oven and electric range off: Yes No Dishwasher off: Yes No Washing machine and clothes dryer off: Yes No

  Comments:_____

ELECTRICAL: All electrical devices off or set as before inspection: Yes No
  Comments:_____

POOL & SPA: Pool equipment set as before inspection: Yes No
  Comments:_____

Smoke detectors, how many? _____ Yes ☐   No ☐   Functional: Yes ☐   No ☐

☐ *The International Association of Fire Fighters (IAFF) is urging households to change more than just smoke alarm batteries. The IAFF also recommends changing to a photoelectric smoke alarm. About 90 percent of homes are equipped with ionization smoke alarms.* https://www.iaff.org/comm/press/102908Smoke.htm

☐ *All Homes with gas appliances should have carbon monoxide detectors installed*

☐ **Although functional at this time (see report), as this report is not a warranty or guarantee, it is strongly recommended that, due to the general condition and/or age of appliances and mechanical components, a home warranty be purchased to safeguard against unforeseen repairs.**

☐ **All repairs involving water intrusion should be checked for mold growth. If mold, mildew, etc., growth exists the proper removal and remediation methods should be utilized to correct the problem.**

COMMENTS: _____
_____
_____

Alert Inspection Service, Inc.

Page   of

Name:

Inspection #

Inspection Address: _____

STRUCTURAL

Foundation Type: Monolithic Slab ☐   Foundation Walls ☐   Columns ☐   Column Type: _____
☐ Condition of accessible areas of the foundation: Acceptable ☐   Unacceptable ☐   Approximate Age: _____
Comments: _____

Site Grading: Level ☐   To house ☐   Away from house ☐
☐ *Exterior ground around perimeter of the structure should be graded to allow water to flow away from the structure. Exterior plants and trees should be trimmed so as not to be in contact with the structure, roof. Fencing, wood siding, and trim that are in contact with the ground will promote moisture damage and pest infestation.*
Comments: _____

CRAWL SPACE	Good	Fair	Poor	Not Inspected	Not Present	Comments
Electrical Outlets						
Electrical Switches						
Floors (Type)						
Walls (Type)						
Insulation (Type)						
Ventilation						
Floor Supports						
Floor Decking						

Comments: _____

EXTERIOR TYPE: One Story ☐   Two Story ☐   Other ☐ _____

EXTERIOR WALLS	Good	Fair	Poor	Not Inspected	Not Present	Comments
Masonry						
Wood						
Trim						
Brick/Stone						
Stucco						
Siding (type)						
Settlement Cracks: Yes ☐ No ☐						
Expansion Cracks: Yes ☐ No ☐						
Retaining Walls: Yes ☐ No ☐						

☐ *All settlement cracks should be monitored periodically to insure that further settlement has not taken place as this inspection does not address any future settlement.*
Comments: _____

WINDOWS: Aluminum ☐   Wood ☐   Awning ☐   Jalousie ☐   Single Hung ☐   Other _____
Caulking Required ☐   Repairs Required ☐   *See Itemized Report* ☐
Comments: _____

DRIVEWAY: Concrete ☐ Asphalt ☐ Pavers ☐   Loose Stone ☐ Other _____
WALKWAY: Concrete ☐ Asphalt ☐ Pavers ☐   Loose Stone ☐ Other _____
☐ *All settlement cracks should be monitored periodically to insure that further settlement has not taken place as this inspection does not address any future settlement. .*
Comments: _____
☐ *Structural components, visible and accessible, for inspection are in good condition.*

Rev. 07152011

7. Settlement Statement (HUD-1)

OMB Approval No. 2502-0265

A. **Settlement Statement (HUD-1)**

B. Type of Loan

1. ☐ FHA 2. ☐ RHS 3. ☐ Conv. Unins.	6. File Number	7. Loan Number	8. Mortgage Insurance Case Number
4. ☐ VA 5. ☐ Conv. Ins.	BLANK2013		

C. NOTE: This form is furnished to give you a statement of actual settlement costs. Amounts paid to and by the settlement agent are shown. Items marked "(p.o.c.)" were paid outside the closing; they are shown here for informational purposes and are not included in the totals.

D. NAME OF BORROWER:

ADDRESS OF BORROWER:
E. NAME OF SELLER:

ADDRESS OF SELLER:
F. NAME OF LENDER:

ADDRESS OF LENDER:
G. PROPERTY LOCATION:

H. SETTLEMENT AGENT:
PH# (941) 366-6660
PLACE OF SETTLEMENT:
I. SETTLEMENT DATE:

J. Summary of Borrower's Transaction		K. Summary of Seller's Transaction	
100. Gross Amount Due from Borrower		**400. Gross Amount Due to Seller**	
101. Contract sales price		401. Contract sales price	
102. Personal property		402. Personal property	
103. Settlement charges to borrower (line 1400)		403.	
104.		404.	
105.		405.	
Adjustments for items paid by seller in advance		Adjustments for items paid by seller in advance	
106. City/town taxes to		406. City/town taxes to	
107. County taxes to		407. County taxes to	
108. Assessments to		408. Assessments to	
109. to		409. to	
110. to		410. to	
111. to		411. to	
112. to		412. to	
120. Gross Amount Due from Borrower		**420. Gross Amount Due To Seller**	
200. Amounts Paid by or in Behalf of Borrower		**500. Reductions In Amount Due to Seller**	
201. Deposit or earnest money		501. Excess deposit (see instructions)	
202. Principal amount of new loan(s)		502. Settlement charges to seller (line 1400)	
203. Existing loan(s) taken subject to		503. Existing loan(s) taken subject to	
204.		504. Payoff of first mortgage loan	
205.		505. Payoff of second mortgage loan	
206.		506.	
207.		507.	
208.		508.	
209.		509.	
209a		509a	
209b		509b	
Adjustments for items unpaid by seller		Adjustments for items unpaid by seller	
210. City/town taxes to		510. City/town taxes to	
211. County taxes to		511. County taxes to	
212. Assessments to		512. Assessments to	
213. to		513. to	
214. to		514. to	
215. to		515. to	
216. to		516. to	
217. to		517. to	
218. to		518. to	
219. to		519. to	
220. Total Amounts Paid by or in Behalf of Borrower		**520. Total Reductions to Amount Due Seller**	
300. Cash at Settlement from/to Borrower		**600. Cash At Settlement to/from Seller**	
301. Gross amount due from borrower (line 120)		601. Gross amount due to seller (line 420)	

U.S. DEPARTMENT OF HOUSING AND URBAN DEVELOPMENT
SETTLEMENT STATEMENT

PAGE 2

L. Settlement Charges

		Paid From Borrower's Funds At Settlement	Paid From Seller's Funds At Settlement
700. Total Real Estate Broker Fees			
Division of Commission (line 700) as follows:			
701.	to		
702.	to		
703. Commission paid at Settlement			
704.	to		
800. Items Payable In Connection With Loan			
801. Our origination charge	$ (from GFE #1)		
802. Your credit or charge (points) for the specific interest rate chosen	$ (from GFE #2)		
803. Your adjusted origination charges to	(from GFE #A)		
804. Appraisal fee to	(from GFE #3)		
805. Credit report to	(from GFE #3)		
806. Tax service to	(from GFE #3)		
807. Flood certification to	(from GFE #3)		
808. to			
809. to			
810. to			
900. Items Required By Lender To Be Paid In Advance			
901. Daily interest charges from to @ /day	(from GFE #10)		
902. Mortgage Insurance Premium for months to	(from GFE #3)		
903. Homeowner's Insurance for years to	(from GFE #11)		
904. years to			
905. years to			
1000. Reserves Deposited With Lender			
1001. Initial deposit for your escrow account	(from GFE #9)		
1002. Homeowner's insurance months @ per month $			
1003. Mortgage insurance months @ per month $			
1004. Property taxes months @ per month $			
1005. Annual assessments months @ per month $			
1006. months @ per month $			
1007. months @ per month $			
1008. months @ per month $			
1009. Aggregate Accounting Adjustment $ <$0.00>			
1100. Title Charges			
1101. Title services and lender's title insurance	(from GFE #4)		
1102. Settlement or closing fee	$		
1103. Owner's title insurance	(from GFE #5)		
1104. Lender's title insurance	$		
1105. Lender's title policy limit $			
1106. Owner's title policy limit $			
1107. Agent's portion of the total title insurance premium	$		
1108. Underwriter's portion of the total title insurance premium	$		
1109. to			
1110. to			
1111. to			
1112. to			
1113. to			
1200. Government Recording and Transfer Charges			
1201. Government recording charges	(from GFE #7)		
1202.			
1203. Transfer taxes	(from GFE #8)		
1204.			
1205.			
1206. to			
1207. to			
1300. Additional Settlement Charges			
1301. Required services that you can shop for	(from GFE #6)		
1302. Pest Inspection	$		
1303. Roof Inspection to	$		
1304. to			
1305. to			
1306. to			
1307. to			
1308. to			
1309. to			
1400. Total Settlement Charges (enter on lines 103, Section J and 502, Section K)			

CERTIFICATION

DATE:

I have carefully reviewed the HUD - 1 Settlement Statement and to the best of my knowledge and belief, it is a true and accurate statement of all receipts and disbursements made on my account or by me in this transaction. I further certify that I have received a copy of the HUD - 1 Settlement Statement.

_____ Borrower   _____ Seller

_____ Borrower   _____ Seller

The HUD-1 Settlement Statement which I have prepared is a true and accurate account of this transaction. I have caused the funds to be disbursed in accordance with this statement.

_____ Settlement Agent   _____ Date

WARNING: It is a crime to knowingly make false statements to the United States on this or any other similar form. Penalties upon conviction can include a fine and imprisonment. For details see: Title 18 U.S. Code Section 1001 and Section 1010.

Page 2 of 3

BLANK2013

8. Listing Agreement

The following is a sample of the Florida Association of Realtors (FAR) Listing Agreement. These forms are set up by FAR to set out the responsibilities of buyers, sellers and Realtors, and are only available to Realtors. We share this extract as a courtesy to inform our readers, should you wish to look at the form in its entirety, you can contact a Florida Realtor.

Exclusive Right of Sale Listing Agreement

Florida Realtors®
The Voice for Real Estate® in Florida

1   This Exclusive Right of Sale Listing Agreement ("Agreement") is between
2*   _____ ("**Seller**") and
3*   _____ ("**Broker**").
4   **1. AUTHORITY TO SELL PROPERTY: Seller** gives **Broker** the EXCLUSIVE RIGHT TO SELL the real and personal property
5*   (collectively "Property") described below, at the price and terms described below, beginning the _____ day of
6*   _____, and terminating at 11:59 p.m. the _____ day of _____, _____
7   ("Termination Date"). Upon full execution of a contract for sale and purchase of the Property, all rights and obligations of this
8   Agreement will automatically extend through the date of the actual closing of the sales contract. **Seller** and **Broker**
9   acknowledge that this Agreement does not guarantee a sale. This Property will be offered to any person without regard to race,
10   color, religion, sex, handicap, familial status, national origin or any other factor protected by federal, state or local law. **Seller**
11   certifies and represents that he/she/it is legally entitled to convey the Property and all improvements.
12   **2. DESCRIPTION OF PROPERTY:**
13*   **(a)** Real Property Street Address: _____
14*   _____
15*   Legal Description: _____
16*   _____ ☐ See Attachment _____
17*   **(b)** Personal Property, including appliances: _____
18*   ....
19*   _____ ☐ See Attachment _____
20*   **(c)** Occupancy: Property ☐ is ☐ is not currently occupied by a tenant. If occupied, the lease term expires _____.
21   **3. PRICE AND TERMS:** The property is offered for sale on the following terms, or on other terms acceptable to Seller :
22*   **(a) Price:** _____
23*   **(b) Financing Terms:** ☐ Cash ☐ Conventional ☐ VA ☐ FHA ☐ Other _____
24*   ☐ **Seller** Financing: **Seller** will hold a purchase money mortgage in the amount of $ _____ with the
25*   following terms: _____
26*   ☐ Assumption of Existing Mortgage: **Buyer** may assume existing mortgage for $ _____ plus an
27*   assumption fee of $ _____. The mortgage is for a term of _____ years beginning in _____, at an
28*   interest rate of _____% ☐ fixed ☐ variable (describe) _____
29*   Lender approval of assumption ☐ is required ☐ is not required ☐ unknown. Notice to **Seller**: You may remain liable for an
30   assumed mortgage for a number of years after the Property is sold. Check with your lender to determine the extent of your
31   liability. **Seller** will ensure that all mortgage payments and required escrow deposits are current at the time of closing and will
32   convey the escrow deposit to the buyer at closing.
33*   **(c) Seller Expenses: Seller** will pay mortgage discount or other closing costs not to exceed _____% of the purchase price;
34   and any other expenses Seller agrees to pay in connection with a transaction.
35   **4. BROKER OBLIGATIONS AND AUTHORITY: Broker** agrees to make diligent and continued efforts to sell the Property until
36   a sales contract is pending on the Property. **Seller** authorizes **Broker** to:
37*   **(a)** Advertise the Property as **Broker** deems advisable including advertising the Property on the Internet unless limited in
38*   (4)(a)(i) or (4)(a)(ii) below.
39   **(Seller opt-out)(Check one if applicable)**
40*   ☐ (i) Display the Property on the Internet except the street address of the Property shall not be displayed on the Internet.
41*   ☐ (ii) **Seller** does not authorize **Broker** to display the Property on the Internet.
42   **Seller** understands and acknowledges that if **Seller** selects option (ii), consumers who conduct searches for listings on
43   the Internet will not see information about the listed property in response to their search.
44*   _____/_____ Initials of Seller.
45   **(b)** Place appropriate transaction signs on the Property, including "For Sale" signs and "Sold" signs (once **Seller** signs a sales
46   contract) and use **Seller's** name in connection with marketing or advertising the Property.
47   **(c)** Obtain information relating to the present mortgage(s) on the Property.
48   **(d)** Place the property in a multiple listing service(s) (MLS). **Seller** authorizes **Broker** to report to the MLS/Association of
49   Realtors • this listing information and price, terms and financing information on any resulting sale. **Seller** authorizes **Broker**,
50   the MLS and/or Association of Realtors® to use, license or sell the active listing and sold data.
51   **(e)** Provide objective comparative market analysis information to potential buyers; and
52*   **(f)** (Check if applicable) ☐ Use a lock box system to show and access the Property. A lock box does not ensure the Property's
53   security; Seller is advised to secure or remove valuables. Seller agrees that the lock box is for Seller's benefit and releases **Broker**,
54   persons working through Broker and Broker's local Realtor Board / Association from all liability and responsibility in connection
55*   **Seller** (_____) (_____) and **Broker/Sales Associate**(_____) (_____) acknowledge receipt of a copy of this page, which is Page 1 of 3 Pages.

ERS-13aa Rev. 11/09 © 2009 Florida Association of REALTORS® All Rights Reserved

Serial#: 000091-200138-6344723

formsimplicity

117 **1.** Dealing honestly and fairly;
118 **2.** Loyalty;
119 **3.** Confidentiality;
120 **4.** Obedience;
121 **5.** Full disclosure;
122 **6.** Accounting for all funds;
123 **7.** Skill, care, and diligence in the transaction;
124 **8.** Presenting all offers and counteroffers in a timely manner, unless a party has previously directed the licensee otherwise in writing;
125 and
126 **9.** Disclosing all known facts that materially affect the value of residential real property and are not readily observable.

127* _____   _____
128 **Date**   **Signature**

129 **9. CONDITIONAL TERMINATION:** At **Seller's** request, **Broker** may agree to conditionally terminate this Agreement. If **Broker**
130 agrees to conditional termination, **Seller** must sign a withdrawal agreement, reimburse **Broker** for all direct expenses incurred
131* in marketing the Property and pay a cancellation fee of $_____ plus applicable sales tax. **Broker** may void the
132 conditional termination and **Seller** will pay the fee stated in paragraph 6(a) less the cancellation fee if **Seller** transfers or
133 contracts to transfer the Property or any interest in the Property during the time period from the date of conditional termination
134 to Termination Date and Protection Period, if applicable.
135 **10. DISPUTE RESOLUTION:** This Agreement will be construed under Florida law. All controversies, claims and other matters in
136 question between the parties arising out of or relating to this Agreement or the breach thereof will be settled by first attempting
137 mediation under the rules of the American Arbitration Association or other mediator agreed upon by the parties. If litigation arises out
138 of this Agreement, the prevailing party will be entitled to recover reasonable attorney's fees and costs, unless the parties agree that
139* disputes will be settled by arbitration as follows: **Arbitration:** By initialing in the space provided, **Seller** (____) (____), Listing
140* Associate (____) and Listing **Broker** (____) agree that disputes not resolved by mediation will be settled by neutral binding
141 arbitration in the county in which the Property is located in accordance with the rules of the American Arbitration Association or other
142 arbitrator agreed upon by the parties. Each party to any arbitration (or litigation to enforce the arbitration provision of this Agreement
143 or an arbitration award) will pay its own fees, costs and expenses, including attorney's fees, and will equally split the arbitrators' fees
144 and administrative fees of arbitration.
145 **11. MISCELLANEOUS:** This Agreement is binding on **Broker's** and **Seller's** heirs, personal representatives, administrators,
146 successors and assigns. **Broker** may assign this Agreement to another listing office. This Agreement is the entire agreement
147 between **Broker** and **Seller.** No prior or present agreements or representations shall be binding on **Broker** or **Seller** unless
148 included in this Agreement. Signatures, initials and modifications communicated by facsimile will be considered as originals.
149 The term "buyer" as used in this Agreement includes buyers, tenants, exchangors, optionees and other categories of potential
150 or actual transferees.
151* **12. ADDITIONAL TERMS:** _____
152* _____
153* _____
154* _____
155* _____
156* _____
157* _____
158* _____
159* _____

160* Date: _____ **Seller's Signature:** _____ Tax ID No: ___ - __ - ____
161* Telephone #'s: Home_____ Work_____ Cell_____ Fax_____
162* Address:_____ E-mail: _____

163* Date: _____ **Seller's Signature:** _____ Tax ID No: ___ - __ - ____
164* Telephone #'s: Home_____ Work_____ Cell_____ Fax_____
165* Address:_____ E-mail: _____

166* Date: _____ **Authorized Listing Associate or Broker:** _____
167* Brokerage Firm Name: _____ Telephone: _____
168* Address: _____

169* Copy returned to **Customer** on the _____ day of _____, _____ by: ☐personal delivery ☐mail ☐E-mail ☐facsimile.

The copyright laws of the United States (17 U.S. Code) forbid the unauthorized reproduction of this form by any means including facsimile or computerized forms.
170* **Seller** (____) (____) and **Broker/Sales Associate** (____) (____) acknowledge receipt of a copy of this page, which is Page 3 of 3 Pages.
ERS-13sa Rev. 11/09 © 2009 Florida Association of REALTORS® All Rights Reserved

Serial#: 008991-200138-6344723

formsimplicity

9. Buyer's Agent Agreement

To see the full version of this form please go to the resources section at

www.InvestmentsInFlorida.com

BUYER BROKER EXCLUSIVE AGREEMENT

THIS BUYER BROKER EXCLUSIVE AGREEMENT (this "Agreement") is made and entered into between:

_____ ("BUYER") and

INVESTMENTS IN SARASOTA ("BROKER").

1. BROKER'S ROLE. BROKER is hereby retained to assist BUYER in acquiring an interest in, or right to use, certain property. BROKER will: (A) consult with BUYER to discuss property requirements, financing alternatives, possession time schedules, financial capabilities, and acquisition and negotiation strategies, (B) assist in obtaining available information of material nature relative to desired properties, (C) make BROKER's best efforts to identify and locate properties suitable to purchase, (D) assist BUYER in presenting and negotiating contract offers on desired properties, and (E) monitor contract and closing deadlines. BUYER understands that other potential buyers may consider, make offers on, or purchase through BROKER the same or similar properties as BUYER is seeking to acquire.

2. BROKERAGE RELATIONSHIP. BROKER has informed and disclosed to BUYER the brokerage relationship between BROKER and BUYER. BROKER's required disclosure notices have been provided to BUYER and the brokerage relationship is

    _____.

3. BUYER'S ROLE. BUYER agrees to: (A) work exclusively with BROKER during the term of this Agreement and be available to evaluate and/or view properties with BROKER, (B) refer to BROKER all inquiries regarding any potential properties for sale, (C) provide reliable information including financial information necessary for the performance of this Agreement, and (D) provide to BROKER general information regarding location, price range, amenities, and any other information needed to help identify desired properties.

4. TERM OF AGREEMENT. BUYER engages and grants BROKER the exclusive right and authority to negotiate for the purchase or other acquisition of a legal or equitable interest in or right to use the real property identified during the term of this Agreement, which shall commence on _____, 20__ ("Commencement Date") and shall terminate on _____, 20__ ("Termination Date"). If BUYER enters into a contract to purchase any property prior to the Termination Date, this Agreement shall automatically be extended until the closing or termination of said contract for sale. If during the _____ day period after the Termination Date, BUYER enters into a contract to purchase any property identified to BUYER during the term of this Agreement, then BUYER will pay the BROKER's Compensation, and this Agreement shall automatically be extended until the closing or termination of said contract for sale.

5. BROKER'S COMPENSATION. Properties listed in MLS provide for BROKER'S COMPENSATION from the Seller. Should the BUYER purchase a property (such as a For Sale by Owner) that does not have provisions for BROKER compensation, BUYER will compensate BROKER in the amount of _____% of the purchase price of each property purchased by BUYER.

6. HOLD HARMLESS. BUYER acknowledges and agrees that BROKER is not an expert in matters including, but not limited to law, surveying, structural conditions, engineering, financing and hazardous materials. BUYER acknowledges that BUYER has been advised to seek professional expert assistance and advice in these and other areas of professional expertise. If BROKER provides to BUYER names or sources for such advice and assistance, BUYER acknowledges and agrees that BROKER does not warrant or guarantee the services and/or products. BUYER also agrees to hold BROKER harmless from liability resulting from incomplete and/or inaccurate information provided by BUYER to BROKER. BUYER agrees to indemnify BROKER against all claims, damages, losses, expenses, or liability arising from the handling of earnest money by anyone other than BROKER.

7. FAIR HOUSING/EQUAL OPPORTUNITY. BROKER shall provide the above services and make properties available to BUYER without regard to race, color, national origin, religion, sex, handicap or familial status as well as any other classes protected under the laws of the United States, State of Florida and applicable local jurisdictions.

8. ATTORNEY'S FEES AND COSTS. In connection with any litigation concerning this Agreement, the prevailing party shall be entitled to recover reasonable attorney's fees and court costs from the non-prevailing party, at all trial and appellate levels.

9. SURVIVABILITY. All provisions of this Agreement which by their nature or context require performance or provide rights after the Termination Date of this Agreement shall survive this Agreement.

10. OTHER TERMS AND CONDITIONS.

    _____

    _____

    _____

    _____

(Buyer's Signature)   (Date)   (Buyer's Signature)   (Date)

(Buyer's Printed Name)   (Buyer's Printed Name)

Buyer's Mailing Address:_____

Buyer's Contact: (Home) _____ (Office) _____ (Cell) _____ (Fax) _____

Email Address: _____ Property Telephone _____

(Authorized Broker's Signature)   (Date)

Brokerage Firm Name: _____ Licensee's Printed Name: _____

ENDNOTES

1. www.eflorida.com/ContentSubpage.aspx?id=52

2. www.theglobeandmail.com/globe-investor/personal-finance/ mortgages/hey-aspiring-snowbirds-the-florida-housing-market-could-be-rebounding/article10737958/

3. Source: FloridaRealtors.org National Association of Realtors

4. business.financialpost.com/2013/01/02/its-not-too-late-to-buy-cheap-property-in-the-u-s-sun-belt/?__lsa=6b7c-7d2f

5. business.financialpost.com/2013/01/02/its-not-too-late-to-buy-cheap-property-in-the-u-s-sun-belt/?__lsa=6b7c-7d2f

6. Canadian Real Estate Wealth Magazine

7. www.realtytrac.com/trendcenter/trend.html

8. www.bizjournals.com/bizjournals/on-numbers/scott-thomas/2012/06/ florida-real-estate-bounces-back-from.html?page=all

9. www.theglobeandmail.com/globe-investor/personal-finance/ mortgages/hey-aspiring-snowbirds-the-florida-housing-market-could-be-rebounding/article10737958/

10. www.theglobeandmail.com / globe-investor / personal-finance/ mortgages/hey-aspiring-snowbirds-the-florida-housing-market-could-be-rebounding/article10737958/

11. higherlogicdownload.s3.amazonaws.com/SOSRAPB/8a3fa275-2c87-4b38-8f56-4bba74a84ce0/UploadedImages/Housing%20Reports%20 March/052013/05.2013%20PBC_SFH_Summary.pdf

12. www.deptofnumbers.com/asking-prices/florida/tampa/

13. www.movoto.com/statistics/fl/fort-myers.htm

14. www.movoto.com/statistics/fl/cape-coral.htm

15. www.naplesarea.com/real-estate-news.asp

16. manausa.com/investment-property-in-tallahassee/

17. bayappraisal.com/blog/

18. www.wftv.com/news/news/local/osceola-co-kissimmee-home-prices-skyrocket-above-o/nX7R2/

17028316R00197

Printed in Great Britain
by Amazon